Think Yourself Safe

How to use your mind to reduce the risk of crime

Tim Reynolds

authorHOUSE®

AuthorHouse™
1663 Liberty Drive
Bloomington, IN 47403
www.authorhouse.com
Phone: 1-800-839-8640

Published by AuthorHouse   05/17/2012

ISBN: 978-1-4685-7869-0 (sc)
ISBN: 978-1-4685-7870-6 (e)

To Linda

For your help, support and encouragement.

CONTENTS

PREFACE

Crime is an emotive subject and very much misunderstood by most people.

In writing this book it is necessary for me to be totally honest with reference to my past and the mistakes that I made when I was young and on the wrong side of the law.

No one can change their past. One can only learn from mistakes and take the corrective actions as appropriate.

To be able to look at crime from both sides of the law with first hand experience of both is a unique occurrence, and one that I have gained throughout my life.

I am not at all proud of my early years and would serve no real purpose going into great detail, but I am truly grateful that I was able to turn my life around.

My last encounter on the wrong side of the law was over thirty five years ago. I have since been involved in security, to a very high level and I hope by writing this that I am able to give an insight into how you are able to reduce the opportunities for crime to happen to you and your loved ones.

NOTE

It is often said that a Leopard cannot change its spots.

We as human beings are not leopards and we do not have spots, but believe me we can change, if we really want to.

INTRODUCTION

You now have in your possession, information that will change your way of thinking about your safety and security forever.

It will train your mind to be less fearful and more confident in your relationship towards crime. Many of the people I have helped overcome their fears and anxiety, have in the past been victims of crime, many have not. They simply wanted more control over their lives and started out wondering how this was possible. If you have ever been the victim of crime there is a high chance that it will happen again unless you take corrective actions, and you can. The good news is this book will show you how to reduce the risk of crime happening to you, your family and friends, to a minimum.

We will look at the world through the eyes of the criminal, we will gain an understanding of what motivates them, why they do what they do and how to avoid becoming their next victim.

Can I really avoid being a victim of crime?

Yes you can. I am not so naïve as to say you will never become a victim of crime even with what I am about to share with you, nor am I wishing to scaremonger anyone or make people more fearful, but a criminal needs one thing, the opportunity to strike. We provide countless opportunities on a day to day basis and we will look at these very directly.

People I have worked with in the past are always amazed how easy it is to take away their opportunities and so avoid becoming a victim of crime. They lead happier and more confident lives because they have control over their circumstances.

The changes they have made have happened by design and not by chance. Now it is your turn.

MY STORY

From my early teenage years and my brushes with the law I knew things had to change. I was at one stage out of control and needed to take corrective actions, and quickly.

To change and turn my life around, I first had to change my way of thinking. I had to look at all alternative ways in which I must change, think and act. I read countless books, studied hard and looked at the world from a different perspective.

This was quite difficult at first, as all change is, and required a little effort on my part. I was surprised how quickly things did change though. I was very pleased with the results and continued from strength to strength. Ironically, I applied for a job as a security officer and was accepted.

What better way to defeat a criminal than knowing how they think, act and are motivated in that direction. I started in supermarkets, arresting people for theft, I was fully trained in how to arrest and in some strange way felt like I had inside information as to what to look out for. I was good at it, very good, so much so that after a year I was made a regional manager looking after a very well known supermarket chains portfolio of twenty seven super stores.

After a couple of years I was offered a very different position in security. This involved working in an International terminal of entry and exit in and out of the UK. I worked along side Special Branch, Immigration, Police fire arms units, International Police, Customs and Excise, British Transport Police and many other organisations. I had to be CTC (counter terrorist checked) and cleared by the home office in London. I was classed as anti-terrorist security. I even began to test security arrangements, posing as a passenger and carrying real Semtex explosives, real guns and weapons through the toughest of security screening measures. Again this was something I was good at, and again I was soon promoted to Managerial Status.

Because of my role in security at that time, I was invited to participate in operation Phoenix. This was the code name for a high security meeting between the English, American and French heads of sate and government along with five hundred dignitaries. For obvious reasons I can not go into details of what happened, but I was proud to be part of the success of operation Phoenix and considered it to be the pinnacle of my security career.

My experiences have given me an insight, from both sides of the law, on what we are doing right and more importantly, what we are doing wrong.

I wish to share with you that knowledge so that you can make your home, your loved ones and possessions safer in today's society, simple practical advice that will change your way of thinking about crime forever.

HOW TO USE THIS BOOK

You will find various exercises in this book that will help you develop a very clear and different way of thinking in the future; sometimes controversial, it will also show you different ways of behaviour that will be safer for you, your friends and family.

Use this book as a reference and come back to it as much as you need to. Do not discard it and leave it on a shelf or lend it to someone and never get it back. It has, by the very nature of keeping you and your family safe, the potential to be literally 'life saving'. Study the mind changing philosophies and notice the changes in your own confidence, awareness and control you will feel from now on.

Before you begin, I would like you to consider how many times in your life you have come close to being a victim of crime (perhaps without even knowing it), or just plain lucky that it hasn't happened to you yet.

If on the other hand you have been a victim, how you wish you had the advantage of foresight, and had studied how you could have reduced the risk to an absolute minimum of it happening in the first place.

Now imagine what it would be like to wake up one morning knowing that you are no longer vulnerable, your anxieties and fears have gone away. You are confident and in control once more.

As you use 'Think Yourself Safe' be prepared to re-evaluate the way you have thought about certain situations in the past, and let go of your old ways of thinking. By thinking in the correct ways that you are going to learn, you will re-programme your mind to keep you safe and free yourself to have a wonderful life.

GETTING STARTED

Ask yourself a question, would you leave a fifty pound note tacked to the bonnet of your car or directly outside of your front door for 12 hours, unattended, with a big arrow sign pointing towards it, and expect it to still be there upon your return?

No!

Why not? Someone would have taken it?

Surly not!

Ask yourself another question, who would you blame for them taking it, yourself or them?

Would you take any responsibility for the loss?

Would you have expected someone else to take care of it for you?

Would you expect society to bring to justice those who took it? Now, no one in their right mind would leave a £50 note for someone to just help themselves, would they?

Everyday, people provide criminals with the opportunity to strike. Not in such an obvious way, but it might as well be to the criminal.

Everyday people leave laptops, hand bags, and valuables on car seats, keys in the ignition. They leave windows open in their homes, doors wide open, expose pin numbers, tell everyone that they are going on holiday and will be away for two weeks. Teenagers walk through parks and dark alley ways at two or three O'clock in the morning. People are exposed to scams and fraudsters; they get mugged, attacked and become victims of crime.

What is going on?

Oh, its ok, the Police are there to protect us!!

Then why do the things that I have described still happen? Firstly, the Police, who I have the utmost respect for and consider their job an impossible task, even these brave men and women can not be everywhere at all times, and secondly, (and this is a bitter pill to swallow), in most cases (I have to stress here that there are always exceptions to this rule), YOU; yes YOU are 50% to blame.

I know at first you will say that it was not my fault; how can I possibly be 50% to blame for becoming a victim of crime.

This is where I am going to be a little cruel to you and say, YES you can.

We must look at the many ways in everyday situations YOU provide opportunities for crime to happen.

Once you realise what you are doing you can guard against it, thwart it and reduce your 50% to a minimum giving you more control.

It is YOU my friend that must take back control and you can, by a shift in your awareness and by using the correct ways of thinking that you are about to discover.

Changes

Nearly everyone I have ever met lives in a comfort zone to some degree, and truly believe that because they did not become a victim of crime today that it will not happen tomorrow.

Trusting to chance like this is a little risky to say the least.

I truly believe that a little knowledge can go a long way, the knowledge and experience I am going to share with you, I hope you will find invaluable. I am not suggesting you change your whole life, just your thinking and awareness.

Start to think about how you would react to certain situations, how to plan for certain scenarios.

What would you really do?

OK, so you have sat in your lounge with a nice cup of tea, and maybe thought to yourself, if I locked myself out or forgot my keys one day how will I get in. You may have even come up with a plan for yourself. Good.

Let me tell you right now, there is not a single burglar that will be sitting in your house drinking tea, thinking how I can get in here.

They will be looking at your home from the outside, and if you have not thought the question through from their eyes, your plan is futile. It is therefore imperative that you change your way of thinking.

Kids these days are always on the internet, and apart from the obvious dangers from undesirable adults etc, are you confident that the information that they freely give away on social network sites is not being used to someone else's advantage, such as when you are all going on holiday and how long your house will be empty for?

You may well have an array of alarms, CCTV equipment or the most up to date electronic devises known to man, but, just like any weapon, these can just as easily be used against you.

You may drive a car and consider yourself an excellent driver, as everybody does. But are you aware you and your car are most at risk when you are stopped at traffic lights?

When we walk along the street we are sending out messages with every step, with our body language and our persona. Is it the right message?

We will look at countless sinarios and situations and gain a greater understanding of why some people fall victim to crime and others do not. Why one house gets burgled while the one next door does not, why and how people every day and in every way innocently provide opportunities for crime to happen.

Once you have the knowledge of how and why this happens, you can change your thinking and awareness to a level where you feel more in control and are not trusting to chance or just wishful thinking.

This is going to require you to change the way you think, act and behave from now on.

There will be changes and every change that you experience will help you develop to a stage where you will feel unstoppable.

SECTION ONE

YOUR HOME

What opportunities are you providing in and around your home?

YOUR HOME

Whether you live in a Caravan, Flat, Bungalow, House or a Mansion, your home should be exactly that, a home. Too much protection could signal that it is a gold mine inside, and always bear in mind that you may need to get out of it quickly in an emergency. Too little protection and it could be an easy target.

Your level of protection should be in contrast to your needs. Only you can decide the level of protection that is right for you. I will give you the perspective from the criminal mindset and an alternative way to look at the problem. I will suggest ways in which you can improve your own security arrangements that will not cost the earth.

CRIMINAL MINDSET

From the outside

The very first thing that a criminal will want to know about your property: Is it going to be worth while to break in here?

What are the chances of getting caught? They will avoid getting caught like the plague.

Secondly; what is known about the occupants? Are you at home or away on a trip somewhere? The criminal may have inside information that you are on holiday or just out for the day, or evening.

How many people live here?

Do you have a regular routine of leaving home for work and returning at the same time?

If caught by you what is you're response likely to be, aggressive, frightened or panic? What resistance will you put up, if any?

Are there any children or pets?

Is it possible to see into the property? The criminal will need to be in and out very quickly, they need to asses entry and exit points.

What physical or psychological barriers are there to hinder their efforts? Can they escape quickly if they need to?

Is there any alarm systems or CCTV cameras?

Are there any nosey neighbours or is it a neighbourhood watch area?

How many people are around going about their daily business, day or night?

How much ambient noise is there?

How many hiding places are there as they approach the property?

What do the doors and windows look like, are they easy to break or unlock?

Is there a garage, sheds or lockable storage boxes? What outside lighting is there?

Is the opportunity great enough to justify the risk? (Is it worth their while)?

These are the questions that a criminal would be asking themselves before attempting a break in. They would be doing this from outside the property and weighing up the risk.

We must now look at what opportunities are being presented and reduce these to a minimum.

REDUCING RISK

From the outside

I want you to stop for a moment, and think about how you would get into your home if you locked yourself out? If your answer is to go to your very trusted friend or relative to collect your spare key, or contact them to bring it to you; congratulations. Any other answer is wrong. Any other answer means that you can get into your home easily, and if you can, so can anybody else.

People have said to me in the past that they would call a locksmith if they had to, but unless you are carrying the correct identification necessary at the time, they will not, and should not change your lock. After all you could be anyone! It is important to stress that if your key holder is going away you should make temporary alternative arrangements, another confidant or a professional key holding service if you are not blessed with too many friends or relatives. Keep the arrangement on a 'need to know' basis, the more people who know who has access to your home the more opportunities you are providing. If you are away on a trip, a night out or on holiday, arrange for your confidant to pop in or house sit.

Timer switches are most useful, turning lights, radios or TV's on and off at strategic times, anyone watching your property will have an enormous task to know whether someone is home or not.

To be able to see into your home is the biggest advantage the criminal has, they will be able to see where the expensive electrical items are, the layout and anything else of interest that may take their fancy. They will already know whether you have satellite TV equipment or not, if you have, you will already be advertising this with a satellite dish on the outside of your property, foolish to compound this by showing them where everything is situated inside by not covering your windows.

Net curtains are very old fashioned theses days, but probably one of the best security measures around. You can see out in the day time, but very difficult for anyone to see in, and that's the way you want it, so if net curtains are not your style, find an alternative that provides the same level of protection.

Children and dogs are, by their very nature, noisy. Noise is good coming from a home (from a security point of view). If children and dogs normally play and make noise in and around your home, then suddenly do not, and the garden has been tidied of all play things the chances are nobody is home and is not likely to be for some time. If you normally leave garden toys on show when just popping out then leave them out if you are going away for any length of time, there is no difference, and it will put doubt in the mind of a criminal.

Record some of the usual noises and use your timer switch to activate the noise at the time the sounds normally come from your home.

Deception is a very useful tool in crime prevention, if you are able to deceive the criminal into thinking 'it's not worth while' you are almost playing them at their own game.

Hedges and fences are very good at providing you with privacy, but they also provide the same for a criminal once they have penetrated that particular barrier. If on the other hand, once a criminal has got over your fence or through your hedge a movement sensor light comes on, or the equivalent, the chances are they will beat a hasty retreat.

If they see that you have an alarm system or CCTV cameras (albeit dummy ones) they will think twice about your property anyway.

Sheds, lockable storage boxes and lock ups are easy targets and are easily protected with inexpensive anti-tamper alarms (just a few pounds). Criminals hate these things.

Why people insist on cluttering up their garages with all the items that they will never use again and leave their second highest value item parked outside on the road is beyond me, but they do. Never the less, keep your garage locked and alarmed also.

Look at your doors and windows, especially the locks; ask yourself if you are able to get into them from the outside, if the answer is yes, then you will need to get them fixed, this may mean a little more expense but security here is the biggest financial outlay you will have to find as it is the most important physical barrier. Ask your local professional locksmith for advice.

Information

Most people I know like to show off a little, they like to tell others of their achievements or up and coming events. They like to tell everyone about their prize possessions, how much they cost, where they keep them, where and when they are going on holiday, their planned nights out at the theatre or cinema and even the fact they keep a spare key under the plant pot. These and many other pieces of prize information are said innocently and mostly to close friends or work colleagues.

I want you to stop again for a moment and think about how much information has been given to you about someone else in a seemingly innocent conversation, someone who you may not even know that well, or even at all. People like to boast about the information they have about other people "Did you know that so and so has got a new car, TV, gold bracelet, is going away on Saturday for a week" etc.

Now this may come as a shock, but what you tell and to who will be told again and again to others. The information that you give to your friends and colleagues will be passed to a much wider audience and quite possibly to people you do not know.

It is nice to be proud of yourself and your loved ones, but guard against giving away too much information that could be counter productive in the wrong hands. Try to keep your information on a 'need to know' basis.

I have been in car showrooms and overheard personal details being given out, names and addresses, followed by polite conversations about holidays, achievements and possessions. I have experienced the same things in hairdressers, post office queues, bus stops, supermarkets, at work, in the street, at social occasions, the list is endless.

As a rule, I would not give away any information that I would not share with one hundred strangers.

All of this happens outside of your home. The protection for your home and all that is in it begins outside, not inside.

It is imperative that you view your home security like the rings of an onion. Beginning with the outer layers and working inwards.

CRIMINAL MINDSET

From the inside

If all has gone well and the criminals were able to break into your property, they would be asking themselves, what goodies are here for me? They would be looking for anything that is of value that they could easily sell on. Everything from high value electrical items like TVs, satellite systems, hi-fi equipment, games consoles, computers, mobile phones, microwave cookers, cameras, video cameras etc. Then any other items that were on offer to them, such as purses, wallets, cash, credit cards, jewellery, car keys (for a quick get away), leather jackets, anything that looks expensive.

Burglars will not care what anything means to you and will not think twice about breaking items, cupboards, or smashing something to get to what they want. They will not care about your family heirlooms or precious photographs that you will never get the opportunity to take again. They have come this far and are keen to get out as quickly as possible.

Invite

A criminal does not necessarily have to break into your home to get inside, sometimes they are invited. I am reminded of a case where a very well spoken and well dressed woman knocked at a door early evening and said that her car had broken down and asked if she could use the telephone to call her husband at the office and offered to pay for the call. Naturally the elderly couple invited her in and gave her the telephone. The woman then dialled the number and apologised as she was put on hold, after several minuets she spoke to her husband and arranged for him to pick her up beside her car, she thanked the couple for their kindness and left some money on the side for the call.

Two months later when the elderly couple received their telephone bill, the call that the woman had made came to over five hundred pounds. It was here own premium rate number, previously set up, at the cost of fifty pounds a minute and was a complete scam. The elderly couple had no choice but to pay the bill, after all they had invited the woman into their home, gave her permission to use the telephone and even offered her a cup of tea.

Fraudsters play on human nature and in some ways devastates lives more than any other criminal.

Other fraudsters include; people pretending to be builders, sales persons, gas or electrical engineers, window cleaners, in fact anyone who comes into your property has the potential to separate you from your money or possessions. The same principle applies to fraudsters; they will have done their homework first, from the outside before attempting the crime on the inside.

We will now look at how we can reduce these opportunities.

REDUCING RISK

From the inside

People have often said to me that they don't have anything worth steeling.

I want you to take a few moments now and look around your home, go into every room. I want you to look at it from a criminal mindset as described in the previous section. Look at what the criminal might see and look for.

Now obviously we have never met, and you may consider that you have a lot or very little worth steeling, what I am sure of is that you will have plenty worth protecting.

Once a burglar has entered your premises, it then becomes a matter of damage limitation. However, you are still able to restrict the amount of loss and damage they do to your home with some simple measures.

If you were to lock and hide everything of value they will only smash and destroy everything trying to find their stash. If on the other hand you were to leave on show, a dummy wallet or purse with a little amount of cash in it along with a couple of old receipts, enough to make it look realistic, an old bunch of keys and maybe an old and no longer used mobile phone just laying around they will truly believe that they no longer need to look for those things, whilst the real ones are placed somewhere safe, and you may wish to play the deception game with other items too, that is for you to decide.

Your high value electrical items should be marked with an invisible ink pen with say, your post code or date of birth and a sticker on show to say that it has been marked; this is always a good deterrent. Never lock internal doors, this will only infuriate and frustrate the criminal who will almost certainly break them open causing even more damage than is necessary.

Confrontation

Statistically, you are more likely to be burgled mid morning than you are in the middle of the night. If you happen to be home when this happens, the actions you should take will depend on whether it is day or night. If this should happen to you in the daytime get out if you can and raise the alarm by making as much noise as possible however possible. If you can not get out and you are confronted by one or more burglars, then your own safety must be your highest priority, do what ever they say, they will not want to see you any more than you do them and they will not want to hang around to long.

If it were to happen when you are in bed asleep, again make as much noise as is possible, but only from your bedroom, call out to other people who may or may not be there, call out their names, this is deception again at its best, shout out that the Police are on their way, if the burglars think they are going to meet with much resistance or get caught they will beat a hasty getaway.

It is of paramount importance that you should NEVER, EVER physically take on an intruder. These people are desperate, maybe on drugs and will have no regard for your safety; they will do whatever it takes to get away and will not think twice about harming you or your loved ones if you confront them.

DO NOT BE A HERO

I have had many physical altercations with criminals in my line of work, and can tell you with absolute certainty that a desperate man, or woman doubles their physical strength and if they do happen to be on drugs they truly become super human.

They may carry weapons such as knives, needles or worse, they will not intend to use these unless they are forced to do so, and your job is, not to force them to do so. Just do what ever they say and they will be gone soon enough. Again you must think damage limitation. Confronting such a situation is harrowing enough without having to deal with physical injury as well.

I have known people to confront burglars with a baseball bat, only to have their weapon of choice used against them.

DO NOT confront burglars on a physical level, but with your mind, for you will be much smarter than they are. It is ok to be frightened, fearful and do as they say, even when they are taking away your possessions. Remember, the number one priority at this stage is your own safety and that of your loved ones.

You can get angry and frustrated after they have gone. It is very rare that 'have a go heroes' come out of the ordeal without injury. This is why businesses from banks to security cash in transit vans train their personnel to do as they are instructed by criminals, not to have a go or try to be heroes. It therefore makes perfect sense that you follow their example.

People say to me all the time that the law allows someone to use 'Reasonable force' to protect their home. Yes, that is quite correct. However, we should bear in mind that the burglar will probably have done his homework first and will be prepared for confrontation should it occur. There may be more than one of them! You will not be prepared for this and you will certainly be on the back foot, placing you at a great disadvantage from the outset. Are you absolutely sure you can win? It may well be the middle of the night and you may only be wearing your night clothes, or less. A confrontation may take place in the kitchen where there are knives ready to hand; children may be standing close by.

Reasonable force is something you are going to have to defend in a court of law. Are you really confident that you wont go 'over the top' and end up with a criminal record yourself? Believe me it has happened on many, many occasions.

Most of the court cases last an eternity, keeping your awareness focused on what has happened, sometimes for years. The stress of that alone is criminal and should be avoided from the outset.

Identification

Your home should be the one place on earth that you are most relaxed. For a lot of people this is where they could be most vulnerable. When you invite anyone into your home, whether it is a salesperson or tradesperson etc, always be aware of any sign things are not right. Never be afraid to ask for identification, to some people this may seem a little rude, but if the person you are asking is genuine they will be more than happy to comply with your request. If after checking their 'id' you are happy to invite them in, monitor their activities, are they going into areas of your home they don't need to?

Do they seem nervous or edgy?

Are they asking questions that they shouldn't?

Is their behaviour conducive to what they are supposed to be doing?

If you are not happy, ask them to leave. If they refuse, they are then trespassing and you will do well to raise the alarm as before.

Another rule I have is never to let anyone into my home that has not pre-arranged the visit.

Friends and family will often frequent your home, and it is quite right that they should. This can happen, very often unannounced. If this is a problem to you, then tell them or make your excuses.

It is your home and you must take full charge of whom, and when people come into it, the only caution that I would recommend with friends and family is the information that you share. This will depend on the level of trust you have with the person/s concerned and only you can decide what you share and with whom.

Identity theft

Identity theft is one of the fastest growing crimes World-wide; again this is all about information sharing. A simple and inexpensive cross paper shredder will stop your discarded rubbish being sort after.

Many people think that when they throw away a piece of paper, such as a bank statement, it somehow disappears forever. But this is not the case; it will always end up somewhere, even if it is the rubbish tip. There are a lot of undesirable people who will deliberately go and look for information in these places, some will even steal your rubbish before it is collected to sift through it and collect the information that they need to steal your identity. Do not be misled in thinking because you have torn the documents up into eight little pieces that people won't go to the trouble to stick them back together, they do. If you have destroyed the relevant documents correctly with a cross-shredder before you throw them away, they will not be able to reassemble the document and all of their efforts will be in vein.

Internet

The internet is yet another way for the criminal to enter your home. If you do not have internet protection you may as well leave your front door wide open and say 'help yourself' It is worth investing a little money on internet security programmes, after all you would do this for your doors and windows, so it makes perfect sense to do this for any other means of criminal opportunity. Again be very wary of what information you are giving away on the internet, social network sites are a haven for gathering information, freely given away to close friends and as I have already stated, people like to boast of what they know about you and will be passing this onto others!

An ex colleague of mine was sacked because he had stupidly placed a picture of himself at a party on the very day he had phoned in sick. The boss got to hear about it from a fellow worker and someone he considered a friend because she wasn't invited.

When you purchase goods via Webb sites, make sure there is a symbol of a golden lock on the payment screen and only then if the company is reputable. If something does not seem right, then do not give your details away.

There are many fraudsters desperately trying to deceive you via the internet and they are extremely clever at what they do. I have even known television journalists to fall for their elaborate tricks, pretending to be their internet provider, Banks or some other well known organisation. Their Webb sites look very convincing and authentic, if a TV journalist can be fooled by these people I would suggest that we all can. So please use extreme caution when using the internet, do your homework first, only use tried and trusted sites for any transactions. Golden rule: If in any doubt, DO NOT USE.

Telephones

Telephones are not exempt from being used by fraudsters either; after all, they are just another means of communicating with you in your home.

An acquaintance of mine (I will call Wendy) received a phone call late one afternoon, the caller said she was from Wendy's Bank and that there had been a major security breach and it was necessary to change everyone's Bank card PIN numbers immediately. The caller asked Wendy, for security reasons, to confirm all of her card details, full name, address, her date of birth and mother's maiden name, Wendy being panicked by the security breach gave the caller all the information she required. The caller gave Wendy a new PIN number to use and thanked her for her co-operation. The very next day Wendy went to her Bank and tried her new PIN number (which of course did not work) so she went inside the Bank only to find her account had been emptied. The caller had sounded so convincing that Wendy was completely fooled by this scam and lost £3,564.00. Now you may think that Wendy had been a little naive to fall for this, but when I tell you that Wendy was a serving Police Officer at that time you may just appreciate how easy it is to fall victim.

Never, Ever give details to anyone especially your PIN numbers no matter how convincing they seem.

SUMMERY

The underline common goal for this entire book is a shift in your awareness and thinking.

I have deliberately started with your home because this is where everything else emanates. It is your native place, your sanctuary in the world. It is here that you should feel most secure, relaxed and at peace.

By looking at ways you innocently provide opportunities for crime to happen in and around your home, and by shifting your awareness and guarding against mistakes you can greatly reduce the threat of crime happening. Making it appear 'not worth while' for the criminal to act gives you control.

By guarding the information you innocently give away, by deception and out-thinking the criminal with your mind and not your money is your first line of defence. This should be prominent and ever present in your thoughts to a point where it is second nature to you. This is not easy to achieve at first, but constant and deliberate consideration to these things will bring about changes in your ways of thinking on a daily basis. Once you do that, you have reduced your 50% towards the opportunity for the crime to happen.

I have not included Alarm systems or CCTV equipment in this section because it is necessary to deal with these at a later stage. (See: The Age of Technology).

EXERCISE

Using the correct ways of thinking that I have described in this section, use the table below and write down 12 ways in which you can make your home less vulnerable that apply specifically to your property and all that it contains. Remember to start listing from the outside and work inwards.

Once you have completed this exercise, consciously look at your list and ask yourself: Am I using the right kind of thinking? Am I on the right track? Go over this section again and compare your list until you are confident.

Twelve ways I can make my property less vulnerable?
1.
2.
3.
4.
5.
6.
7.
8.
9.
10.
11.
12.

SECTION TWO

YOUR CAR

My Car, My Pride and Joy!!

YOUR CAR

Your car is an extension of yourself to some degree. These days' people make general assumptions about a person by what type of car they drive, rich, poor, young, old, male or female etc.

As we go about our daily lives we are giving off signals all of the time with our body language. Subconsciously, we do exactly the same when we drive. Do we drive aggressively, passively, with purpose or just dawdling along without a care in the world? What opportunities are you providing to criminals with your vehicle?

Firstly, it must be noted that nearly all car crime is opportunist and happens on the spur of the moment and is rarely pre-meditated.

Sat-Nav (Satellite Navigation Systems)

Sat-Nav's are a wonderful invention for getting you from A to B. If you happen to own a portable one, they are highly sort after by criminals. Whilst it makes perfect sense to hide these away and out of sight while you are not in your vehicle there may be tell-tale signs that one is in your vehicle from the little circle marks left on your windscreen. Try to get into the habit of wiping these marks from your windscreen with a cloth every time you detach your Sat-Nav. It is not only sufficient to take your Sat-Nav with you because if a criminal suspects that there is a Sat-Nav in the vehicle they will try to break in anyway.

By far the biggest problem with Sat-Nav's (portable or built in) is the fact that they have a function screen 'My Home' when pressed or activated will direct you from wherever you are to your front door as you will probably have entered your home address as directed. It would be bad enough for you to have your vehicle stolen while away from home, but to have the criminal turn on your Sat-Nav and go direct to your home and burgle it because they have perfect directions and knowing full well you are not there would be catastrophic. Unfortunately this has happened on many occasions and the criminals have even stolen the keys to the vehicle a couple of times where the front door keys were on the same bunch as the vehicle keys, they didn't even have to break in, they simply opened the front door and helped themselves.

A friend of mine recently celebrated his birthday and was given a Sat-Nav as a present. He was speaking to me about his Sat-Nav and asked me how it all worked; I was able to show him and gave him what turned out to be a good piece of advice.

His car was stolen while he was at his local supermarket, he realised it was missing almost immediately as he had only popped in to get his lottery ticket, the car thieves naturally found his Sat-Nav and made their way to the 'My home' page. Acting on my advice my friend had made his 'My home' address the local Police station. A quick call from my friend on his mobile phone to the local Police alerted them just as two youths arrived at the Police station in my friend's car. You can only imagine the look on their faces as they were both arrested and taken directly into custody.

My friend got his car back the next day without a scratch on it.

It makes perfect sense to make an alternative address close to where you live your 'MY home' page, if you know your way home from your local Police station, all the better.

On Show

Criminals will walk past your vehicle when it is parked and look for any opportunity they may be able to take advantage of.

Now I know this may seem an obvious statement, but, if you leave anything on show that will be of any value to a criminal, expect to have it stolen. I am amazed how often this happens. Everything from handbags, wallets, laptops, briefcases, loose change, shopping, in fact anything you can imagine still gets left on car seats in full view. I have even known secret military documents to go missing from a car because it was left unattended in a petrol station for just a few moments, and unbelievably, with the car unlocked.

Hide everything away all of the time; do not leave anything on show. I cannot stress enough that if you leave anything on show and in full view, you are providing an opportunity for the criminal to take it. And they will.

Setting Off

Before you embark on any journey, make sure the area around your car is safe.

Criminals know that it will take you a few moments to get into and start your car, adjust the seat belt, turn the radio down, check mirrors etc. You may be vulnerable at this point to 'car jacking' (mugged of your car and keys). If the area is not safe and you are not comfortable with people that may be hanging around for no apparent reason, walk on past to a safe distance and call the Police from your mobile phone, if you do not have a mobile phone, go into any public building, shop, garage, or anywhere else that may be to hand and ask to use their phone to call the Police. Do not take chances, if you have read the situation wrong and it turns out to be all very innocent, then that's fine. You may feel a little embarrassed, but you will be safe and unharmed.

While Driving

This is probably the one area where everyone has broken the law at least once. It may have only been driving at 32miles an hour in a 30mile an hour speed limit and you may not have been caught, or even been aware you were going that particular speed at that time, but it is still breaking the law.

There has been a recent case of an elderly gentleman prosecuted for blowing his nose while stopped at a set of red traffic lights; the charge was not being in control of his vehicle and so driving without due care and attention.

The laws of the highway can be so complicated sometimes that we can never be sure if we are breaking the law or not.

There are however, many people that clearly have no regard for the law or other road users and continually and blatantly break the law knowingly. These people assume that the law does not apply to them. Drivers like these are the perpetrators and cause of 'Road Rage'

Our vehicles are an extension of our own personal space, if someone invades that space by 'cutting us up' or causing us to swerve, we get angry or frustrated we too can suffer a little 'Road Rage' or anger towards a fellow road user.

Most people want to get from 'A to B' as quickly as possible these days and the whole experience can be very stressful. It is other drivers getting in our way and not driving to our own exacting standard (whatever that may be) that causes the stress.

I want you to stop again now and think of a time when you made another driver angry to the point where they tooted their horn or gestured rudely towards you in an angry way. I also want you to think of a time where a situation made you fearful.

We have all experienced this to some degree. Our reaction to these situations will decide whether we are providing an opportunity for a violent confrontation or not.

Another question; Have you ever walked along a busy pavement and someone walking towards you has stepped to one side to let you pass and at the very same moment, with split second timing, you have stepped to the very same side to let them pass and you end up doing a side step shuffle together that would grace the 'Hot Shoe Show'? What was the outcome? The chances are that you both laughed it off, apologised to one and other and went on your way. It naturally follows that you should have the same frame of mind when driving.

As with everything else, our ethos must be a change in our thinking.

When driving, it is imperative that you are relaxed. Does it really matter if you are five minuets late, if it does, then leave earlier? Put on some relaxing music, if someone causes you to get angry by doing what you may consider something stupid, check your emotions and remember a time when you probably done the same. If you are the cause of someone getting angry at you to the point where they toot and gesture at you, look at them, smile and apologise (situation de-fused immediately).

I used to be a terrible driver in my younger days, I used to think that I literally owned the road and everybody else was an inconvenience being there. No one used to let me out of turnings or give way to me, It was always imperative that I reached my destination in record quick time. I never had an accident and of course thought I was the best driver in the world and everyone else was just idiots. It was of course ME that was the idiot. Other road users have just as much right to be on the road, there are good drivers and not so good drivers. There are drivers that may not have much experience or be new to the area and not know where they are going. But as long as they are legal they have every right to be there. I now drive in a positive but courteous, considerate and friendly manner. I am never late, I do not get tooted or gestured at, I am let out of turnings and people give way to me all of the time. I thank people when they let me out or give way as I do this to others. I also apologise if for what ever reason I happen to annoy someone and do not let them ruin my day. If there is a hold up, so what, it is part of everyday driving and there is nothing I or anyone can do about it. Now this may seem idyllic, but if you adopt the same driving mentality, you would be very, very unlucky to be the victim of 'Road Rage', either your own or somebody else's and so avoiding the opportunity for physical confrontation.

When Stopped

You are most vulnerable in a vehicle when stopped; this could be at traffic lights, roundabouts or just a queue of traffic.

There are thief's who rely on the fact you will have to stop at a set of traffic lights. They lay in wait and are more than capable of taking quick advantage of whatever opportunity you happen to be providing.

A few years ago, my area manager who was an ex Scots Guard, six foot two tall and just as wide, used to drive an enormous amount of miles per week. On his way home on a glorious summer evening he had his driver's window down to let in some cool air. He was rather flamboyant in his ways and always wore expensive jewellery. The rush hour traffic was heavy as he pulled up at a set of traffic lights, he rested his arm on the open window and as quick as a flash the little finger on his right hand was clamped with a pair of pliers, he was in excruciating pain and was robbed of all his jewellery. He was also hit on the head and suffered a cut above his right eye. He had not been aware of his surroundings and totally unaware of the three males that had robbed him and made off just as quick. Working in the security industry he should have known better, and of course we all gave him the usual amount of 'sympathy' once he had recovered. When stopped at traffic lights, roundabouts, traffic hold ups or for any other reason it is imperative that you have your wits about you, your awareness must be at its highest at this point. Never pull up behind a vehicle so close that you can not get out of the space you are in if you need to. Always allow what I call 'escape space' if you have checked your mirrors and all around you and feel threatened for whatever reason you are then able to manoeuvre out of your current position to safety. Keep your windows up while stopped and always keep your doors locked.

Parking

Always park in a well lit area, bear in mind that if you park during day light hours, it may not be very well lit on your return at night. Try to park under a street light if possible or a secure area at least.

One time when I went to the theatre in London, I parked in what I thought was a very secure location, very busy and a friendly area. Upon my return that night I found that my car was the only one around and the whole area was a hive of youthful activity and very daunting to say the least. Everything was fine, but if I had been a lone female at that time it would have been a very scary situation.

It is worth while checking parking facilities if you are going out of town or an unfamiliar location before you go.

Breakdowns

Breaking down is largely avoidable if you have your vehicle serviced on a regular basis and you carry out routine checks like oil, water and tyre pressures etc. However if you are unlucky enough to break down, you are again vulnerable.

Possibly one of the best insurances you will ever buy is breakdown cover. It guarantees you assistance if the worst were to happen and you breakdown.

Unless you have run out of petrol/diesel when you breakdown, you are normally able to drive just a short distance to relative safety. If your tyre is flat, a few more hundred yards will make no difference at all, if the engine is making 'funny noises' the same will apply.

Modern day vehicles are fitted with early warning lights to warn of anything wrong with your vehicle, always pay attention to these and make your way to a safe place before stopping.

Accidents

Tempers can run high when an accident occurs. Arguments will inevitably be exchanged as to who was to blame. This can sometimes lead to physical exchanges; this is to be avoided at all costs, if you are fortunate enough to be unharmed in the collision it would be madness to suffer injury because of a physical exchange.

If you feel vulnerable at the scene of an accident and are able to still drive, then go to the local Police station and report the accident straight away, if you are unable to drive, call the Police immediately or ask someone else to call them on your behalf. Insurance companies ask you not to admit liability or blame for the accident, it is however acceptable to apologise and play the confused or injured party until the Police arrive, this will keep you out of trouble and avoid arguments or physical confrontations.

This is deception again but will reduce any opportunities that you may provide for a confrontation.

Your Legal Obligation

If you are involved in an accident which causes damage or injury to another person, vehicle, animal or property, you MUST:

- Stop
- Give you're own and the vehicle owner's name and address, and the registration number of the vehicle, to anyone having reasonable grounds for requiring them.
- If you do not give your name and address at the time of the accident, report the accident to the Police as soon as reasonably practicable, and in any case within 24 hours.

Law RTA 1988 sect 170

- If another person is injured and you do not produce your insurance certificate at the time of the accident to a Police officer or to anyone having reasonable grounds to request it you MUST:
- Report the accident to the Police as soon as possible and in any case within 24 hours
- Produce your insurance certificate for the Police within seven days.

Law RTA 1988 sect 170

Correct at time of publication.

SUMMERY

In most cases your vehicle will be the second highest value item that you pay for or own after your property. It is therefore necessary to create the same impression as you would for your home, make it appear 'not worth the risk' to break into, steal from or attack.

Avoid leaving anything on show.

Drive in a confident, positive, considerate and relaxed friendly manner.

Pay attention to areas in which you park. Make sure your vehicle is roadworthy.

Carry out regular maintenance checks and servicing.

Be aware when going to and from your vehicle of any dangers there might be.

Have awareness around you whilst driving of vehicles three or four ahead and behind you.

Again, we must reduce the opportunities that we provide for crime to happen.

As we have seen we can only achieve this by a shift in our awareness, thinking and acting in the right way.

EXERCISE

This time, using the table below write down 10 ways in which you can make yourself and your vehicle less vulnerable that apply specifically to you and your vehicle and all that it contains.

Once you have completed this exercise, consciously look at your list and ask yourself: Am I using the right kind of thinking?

Go over this section again and compare your list until you are confident.

Ten ways I can make myself and my vehicle less vulnerable?
1.
2.
3.
4.
5.
6.
7.
8.
9.
10.

SECTION THREE

YOU

The most valuable asset you have

We now come onto the most important and complicated subject of our study, and possibly the most overlooked YOU!!

Most people care more about their possessions than they do themselves. If their car, television, computer or other prize possession starts to falter, they panic or get angry and repair or replace it as soon as they can. If on the other hand they start to falter themselves physically they will put off going to the doctors for as long as they can. In many ways this is largely due to the fact we consider ourselves to be indestructible and have no comprehension of how vulnerable we can be physically or mentally until something bad happens.

As we go about our daily lives we truly believe that nothing bad will happen to us and most of the time our guard is down because of this way of thinking.

We probably provide more opportunities for crime to happen to ourselves than in any other area of our lives, and it is here that we must now base our attentions.

I want you to study the list of people below:

Name	Occupation	Age	Hobbies	Lives in
Bob Smith	Welder	42	Clay Shooting	Cornwall
Nancy Wright	Secretary	29	Gym	Surrey
Ryan Jennings	At School	14	Football	Manchester
Nelly Pearce	Retired	76	Book reading	Birmingham
Nathan O'Rourke	Unemployed	19	Drink / Drugs	Newcastle
Denise Odenusi	Social Worker	51	Cinema / Films	London

Based on the information that you already have about each of these people, I want you to complete each of the boxes below with a *Yes, No, Good, Average* or *Poor* answer:

Name of person	Lives alone?	Social life?	Financial wealth?	Fitness levels
Bob Smith				
Nancy Wright				
Ryan Jennings				
Nelly Pearce				
Nathan O'Rourke				
Denise Odenusi				

Now picture in your mind what each one of these people would look like, what they would be dressed in, colour of skin, hair colour and length, short, tall, round or thin? Would they talk with a local accent? What mode of transport would they use? Are you able to build a picture in your mind of their life style?

What you have just done, and with only four small pieces of information on each of our subjects is profiled them. You could by now even tell what sort of persona or body language they would each have.

This also works in reverse. The persona and body language that we all give off all of the time tells others an incredible amount about us.

Some body language experts believe that the information that we have just assumed about our fictitious subjects can be assumed about you with just a single glance.

Now ask yourself which of our subjects would be most vulnerable to attack? Who would put up most resistance in any given situation that you can think of?

As incredible as it sounds, the account that follows actually happened.

On a rainy morning in 1979 in a well know town in north Kent, two men pulled up on a motor bike outside a post office wearing motor bike leathers and full faced crash helmets. They ran into the post office brandishing one sawn off shotgun and one pistol, they demanded that the post master hand over all the cash. They pushed an elderly lady aged 72 out of the way to get to the counter. The elderly lady, later known as 'ave a go Edna' was overcome with rage, she started hitting the two men with her umbrella, now this must have looked like a scene from a comedy show, the two men were cowering as the umbrella blows rained down on them. They tried to escape through the front door, but Edna wouldn't let them go anywhere, four builders that had just come out of the breakfast café next door joined in the affray and were able to pin the two criminals to the floor until the Police arrived.

The two men were given custodial sentences for armed robbery. Edna and the builders were given posthumous bravery awards, and the postmaster had to repair a hole in his ceiling where the shotgun had 'gone off'.

Edna and Co were lucky that day and I would never endorse having a go by anyone, however it proves that you do not have to be six foot six tall and an international rugby player to fend off an attacker.

In this instance, the criminals knew only to well that whatever they did, they would not win. If they harmed an elderly lady they would be in for a really hard time later on down the line.

Edna had turned a situation where the two criminals thought it 'worth while' into one that was not so.

As with your home and your car, you must convey the impression with yourself that it would not be worth while for a criminal to attack, mug or steal from you.

Regardless of your age, fitness, strength or gender you are capable of giving off the right or wrong signals. We achieve this through our body language and overall persona.

Whilst body language is an exact science and takes a long time to study and master, there are general perceptions that we can observe and put into practice immediately.

We all read body language every minute of our day (subconsciously), to be even better and gain a greater understanding of this fascinating subject try watching television with the sound turned down. The chances are that after a short while you will be able to follow the script quite well, this works especially well with soap operas and films. Expand on this and observe people in the street or in public places, or as I call it 'people watching'. You will be amazed at what you can pick up from their body language after a short while and with practice, you will soon be able to tell if someone is timid or confident, strong willed or meek and mild.

The Laws of Nature

There are certain laws of nature that apply to us humans as well as the animal kingdom. The strongest will survive. Or to put this another way: the weakest are the most vulnerable, and appearances count for everything. The stronger an animal looks the less likely it is to be attacked or dominated, the higher it holds its head the stronger it appears to be. Any sign of weakness will be taken advantage of. Any sign of strength will be respected.

These laws apply to you, as an example, if you walk slowly along the pavement shuffling your feet looking at the ground, shoulders down, what signals are you omitting? If on the other hand you walk with purpose, head held high with the persona of a king the opposite effect is achieved.

Simply put, if you make yourself an easy target, someone will take advantage of you.

Always convey the persona of *'Don't even think about it'*.

Only you will know your own life style that you will be able to carry this way of thinking onto.

Fake It Till You Make It

A lot of people have said to me in the past, "I can't do this; it's un-natural for me to be someone or something that I'm not"

As the great Henry Ford once said, "If you think you can or you think you can't, either way you are probably right"

The easiest way to change is to pretend or fake it at first, and very soon it will become second nature to you. Practice being a confident, positive and self-assured person, yes, again this may require a little effort but you will soon be giving off the right signals and feel more in control in every situation.

Danger Areas

There are many danger areas to be avoided.

It saddens me greatly when I hear on the news that a teenage girl has been attacked while walking home alone from a night club through the local park or alley way. Why oh why did she put herself in such a vulnerable position. And why does this sort of thing happen again and again? This is of course only one such example, and there are far too many to list here, but we should all be aware of putting ourselves in such positions.

The most unpredictable and dangerous situations occur when alcohol is involved. The effects of alcohol varies greatly from person to person from violent behaviour to down right stupid, but one thing is for sure, alcohol changes everyone's way of thinking and behaviour. Most people develop a more 'care free attitude' Nothing can hurt me and I can do no wrong. Normal, rational and respectable people of all ages sometimes turn into monsters. Now I like a drink as much as the next person, and yes I have been known to have one too many in the past, as I suspect we all have, and yes I admit that I have woken up the next morning and given myself a good talking to for being so stupid. However, I have never committed a crime or got myself into a dangerous situation through alcohol. This is largely down to the fact that when I sense a situation turning bad, I simply walk away. I have been only too aware of the effects of alcohol in my line of work, dealing with drunken people as a job and when you are sober is quite different from trying to make sense of it all when you are under the influence as well.

There is a very famous film where an old Japanese man is teaching a young student the art of Karate, they discus the merits of avoidance and the old Japanese man tells the young student in his Japanese accent, "The best way to avoid punch, is no be there"

To my mind there is no better piece of advice ever said or written than that. The best way to avoid a dangerous situation is not to be there when it happens. If you are constantly studying the areas and people around you and conscious of any dangers, you can simply walk away.

You have the ability to change your surroundings or opportunities you may be providing at any time.

When I was younger I was walking home from football practice one evening, I was very conscious of three older boys hanging around on a street corner, as I passed them one of them noticed that I had a very expensive pair of football boots slung around my neck, they started to follow me, so I walked quicker, the quicker I walked the faster they came behind me. I was very tired after my football practice and knew that I would not be able to out-run them. By this time they were only a few yards behind so I quickly darted into the nearest house entrance and rung the bell. The older lads thought that I must live there and walked past and on their way. The door was answered by a man still eating his tea, I asked him if Tom was in, he of course replied that there was no Tom at this address, I engaged him in conversation of where Tom might live and described Tom to him until I was satisfied that the older lads were gone, I then made my apologies and went another route home. Tom of course was completely fictitious, but that didn't matter. I was safe. I had found a safe haven or an escape hatch as I like to call it.

We are normally surrounded by escape hatches most of the time. Escape hatches are places, buildings or surroundings that by their very nature would deter a criminal from carrying out an attack or crime. If you do not have a convenient escape hatch and begin to feel vulnerable you must get out of that situation, and quickly, find an escape hatch area. Leave the pub or club, get off the train or bus early, and simply walk or move away.

Drugs

I have never taken drugs, and cannot comment on how they pretend to make you feel. I have known and dealt with many people that have, most of which are now dead. My advice with drugs is very simple. Have nothing to do with them. Do not go where drugs are likely to be, do not associate with people who 'do drugs'. Drugs kill and harm more people than all the knife and gun crime put together. I repeat, have nothing to do with drugs.

Simple but Effective

There are many observations that I have made over many years of people when they are 'out and about' providing the most basic opportunities for crime to happen, almost to the point of invite. I would like to share a few of these with you now to give you just a flavour of pure vulnerability.

- Women who leave their handbags on top of shopping trolleys in the middle of the shopping isle unattended while they go looking for the bargains.
- People who speak their pin number as they punch it into the card machine when paying for goods.
- People when getting onto a train, place their cases or bags directly above the seat they are sitting, and are unable to keep a clear view of them.
- Men opening wallets in public places and showing the world and his wife the bundle of notes that are in there.
- People leaving laptops on café tables while they go to the loo.
- People leaving mobile phones unattended on bar tops, table tops and other vulnerable places.
- People walking down the street alone with the most up to date and expensive mobile phone to their ear.
- Teenagers that wear back packs and leave the zipper open behind their view, exposing their purses and phones.
- Open handbags at anytime, anywhere.
- Young women leaving unattended drinks in night clubs. (Date rape vulnerable).
- Young women walking home at night alone.
- Young men walking home at night alone.
- Wallets sticking out of men's trouser pockets.
- Cameras, video cameras or any other expensive electronic equipment being left unattended or on show.
- Expensive jewellery being worn at an inappropriate time or place.
- Push bikes being left unsecured.

The list could go on and on, and you could by now add several of your own. If you can, that's great because you are now starting to think in the correct way.

SUMMERY

Awareness is the key. Awareness of your surroundings and people around you.

The other key element to your safety, and equally important is, avoidance.

Avoiding people, places and situations that have the potential to perpetrate violence, theft or any other form of criminal activity. Study body language; look for signs that things are not right. If in doubt always listen to what some people call your 'Gut Instinct' it is natures way of telling you to 'fight or flight' every animal has this built in response to danger. Learn to listen to it; it is our natural defence mechanism. When you have these feelings, never fight; always remove yourself from the situation.

If your possessions are ever damaged or stolen, you may get angry or emotional, but you can replace them eventually.

You must never allow yourself to be, physically or mentally harmed because of criminal activity or violence, you my friend are irreplaceable. You cannot go out and buy another you. There are no spare parts, no re-wind of events.

Hindsight is a wonderful thing, (I wish I had done this or that instead). Foresight on the other hand is what we do have, given the right way of thinking. You are being introduced to the right way of thinking. Use it well.

EXERCISE

For this exercise, write in the table below, 6 examples of times from your past when you have been in a possible danger situation. Go back as far as you need to. No need to write the whole experience, just a 'headline' to remind you of the time, place or situation.

Six examples of danger situations from my past.
1.
2.
3.
4.
5.
6.

Now take each example, and using your new way of thinking, go over in your mind how you would have dealt with each situation differently.

Ask yourself, if I was in that same situation tomorrow, would I feel confident of the outcome? If your answer is 'no' then go over this section again until you are confident.

SECTION FOUR

ON HOLIDAY

Are We There Yet?

ON HOLIDAY

So, you are going on holiday, the sun will be shinning, there will be lots of people having fun, everyone will be in a good mood, lots of food and drink, not a care in the world, the kids are already asking "are we there yet"?

What could possibly go wrong?

When I worked at the international terminal of exit and entry into the UK, there was the inevitable amount of holiday travellers. The amazing fact for us was the amount of holiday makers that turned up without one of the big three: Passport, Tickets or Money. There were other forgotten items as well, such as Spectacles, Walking sticks, Handbags, Suitcases, False teeth, Ski's, Golf clubs, wheelchairs. There was even a 9 year old girl that was literally left behind.

We used to have a saying, that when people go on holiday, they shut their front door and leave their brains inside.

As cruel as this sounds, in many cases it's true.

It is quite right and correct that when you go on holiday, whether it is at home or abroad, it should be a fun and relaxing time. However this is a time when you should also be even more aware of your surroundings. You are now very much out of your comfort zone, you need to be even more 'switched on'.

Care free holiday makers are probably the most vulnerable people world wide.

Have you ever noticed that in any tourist place anywhere in the world, the price of anything nearly doubles? This is purely based on the fact that a tourist on holiday 'doesn't care'. They are there for one thing, and one thing only, a good time, nothing else matters. Money doesn't matter, possessions and safety doesn't matter any more! For a criminal, this is the Cup Final, the Lottery Win, the Moon Landing, the Promised Land, and Utopia. To have the abundance of so many people in one place at one time and with so much, without a care in the world or an ounce of awareness between them is their dream come true.

I am not a betting man, but I would bet you (a friendly handshake bet) that you know of at least one person who has had at least one thing stolen whilst they were on holiday.

When you go away on a trip or on holiday, pack everything that you would normally take with you, make sure you take a fun loving attitude with you, but please don't leave your awareness and correct thinking behind. If you do you may have just as well left your front door wide open (and believe me that's been done as well).

Let's now have a look at some essential things we need to be aware of, so that we do not have to make any embarrassing excuses or insurance claims upon our return.

Leaving Home

If you do not normally use a check list before going away on holiday, now may be a good opportunity to start. Not only does it remind you of essential things you must do, but also eases the stress and pressure before you set off. Draw up a list of all the things that you would normally do before you go and cross them off as you do them. In addition to your list, check the do's and don't list below.

Don't:

- Tell anyone that you are going away, unless they need to know.
- Make it obvious that your home is unattended.
- Leave an answer message on your phone saying that you are away.
- Leave a 'gone on holiday' messages on your e-mail.

Do:

- Arrange for a house sitter or a close friend or relative to keep an eye on your property while you are away, closing/opening curtains etc.
- Cancel newspaper and milk deliveries.

- Set all automatic timers/ switches.
- Lock all doors and windows.
- Lock all garages and out buildings.
- Set all alarm systems. (If appropriate).
- Make sure that any responses to alarms are correct.
- Ensure that your mail cannot be seen 'Piling up' on a door mat.
    If it can, have your mail re-directed or held by the Post office until you return.
- Make sure your travel arrangements are in hand well in advance.
- Check your vehicles maintenance (if you are taking one) before you go.
- Check that you have all the correct documentation, money, tickets, passports etc.
- Allow adequate time for your journey.

Airports/Docks/Terminals

Once you arrive at the airport or any other place of departure, your stress levels will almost certainly rise due to 'information overload' and the sheer amount of people in these places.

You have to park the car, find your shuttle bus, steer the luggage trolley with the wonky wheel, find the check in desk, negotiate security, buy magazines, purchase the duty free, try to keep everyone together in one group, go back to security because you've left something behind, try as hard as you can to find a screen with your departure number on it, make sure everyone goes to the loo, realise that you all have just ten minuets to walk 1.5miles to your departure gate, go through your hand luggage again to find everyone's passports and tickets, calm little Lucy because she does not like planes, boats or trains, stop little Johnny from hitting the man sitting behind you with his colouring book, and in addition to all this chaos I am asking you to raise your awareness and think correctly because you are at your most vulnerable!! Whoa!! Back up back up.

For many people this is normal. I have known people to get to their destination and complain bitterly that their luggage hasn't arrived, filled out all of the appropriate forms and set the wheels in motion for claims against the airline, have their holidays ruined because they have no clothes, give holiday reps a nervous breakdown, return home, only to find that their suitcase was in the boot of their car all along.

I would now like to introduce you to the 6 Ps:

Proper **P**rior **P**lanning **P**revents **P**oor **P**erformance.

While a lot of my colleagues and associates consider this to be a life skill, it is most prevalent when going on holiday or a trip.

I draw your attention back to the last item on our Do's list. Allow adequate time for your journey. It is easy to see that the situations mentioned above, however comical, can not only make people vulnerable but place them and others in great danger, and its all because of the lack of adequate time and proper planning.

Going on holiday is not something we do every day, so it makes perfect sense to plan properly, give yourself more than double the time that you need, relax, be aware of your surroundings, people watch and enjoy the experience.

Boats, Planes & Trains

Let's face it; whatever the mode of transport, all most people want to do is just get there. They don't want delays or hold ups of any kind.

Some people are very nervous travellers, not helped by the fact that the very first thing they see when they arrive at their airport/port is the word 'Terminal' followed by 'Departures'. Some are very exited and some frustrated for whatever reason, smokers get really tetchy having to go many hours without a cigarette. This tends to be a time when a lot of people behave in ways they would not normally behave, especially if they have had a stressful journey getting to the port of departure.

All of this uncharacteristic behaviour and the very quick invitation to partake in alcohol once you are under way, has, in the past, led to 'Boat, Train or Air-rage'.

What is the first thing that most people do when confronted with rage or temper? They get angry and aggressive as well.

Now you don't need a degree in Rocket Science to realise that with so many people trapped in a box on water, on the track or in the air with no way out, that a situation of this kind has the potential to be, a little dangerous.

This is where Stewards/Stewardesses come into their own.

They are highly trained and skilled in dealing with these situations and do not need any assistance/interference from well meaning members of public. If this should ever happen in or on your chosen means of transport, you may not be able to remove yourself from the situation physically, but you can psychologically.

Remain calm, do not get involved and leave it to the professionals.

If the rage is directed at you for any reason, do as you would do when driving, simply apologise and move away, try to understand that the person directing their rage at you may not have the benefit of the 6 Ps and is probably in a state of chaos. The calmer you are the calmer people around you will be.

Any behaviour attracts like behaviour, so remain calm at all times and enjoy your journey; it is an integral part of your holiday after all.

Arrivals

When you arrive at your destination airport/port, you will notice that there will be a stampede to get off the mode of transport that you are on. To get involved in this game of 'must get to where my luggage is first' is not one I recommend, again people's stress levels rise to the point of panic and then wonder why they look suspicious going through customs!

You are on holiday for a reason, to relax and enjoy the experience.

Take your time, someone has to be last onto the transfer coach, it might as well be you.

You're Destination

Great, you've arrived; time to check in to your accommodation. Now you will be tired, hungry and your mental faculties will be at their lowest. You may be asked for your credit/debit card details. If you are abroad you may be asked to produce your passport again for the umpteenth time of your journey, you will have to fill out and sign forms and possibly wait for porters or be given directions that you won't understand.

You will be trying to absorb as much as you can about your surroundings and all the information you are being given about breakfast, bar opening and closing times etc! And all you want to do is get to your room!

Once you have eventually arrived at your room, the chances are that you will have been given an electric card to open your door instead of an old fashioned key.

Please do not be surprised to find that it doesn't work and you will have to go back to reception so they can update it on their system, they will then ask you to try it again, and it normally works after about the fourth time of trying. Allow between 15 to 20 minuets for this depending on how far reception is from your room.

With all of the confusion, it will come as no surprise to discover that you have just given a £20 tip to someone who didn't deserve it instead of the £2 that you had intended in what ever currency it may be.

Ask yourself, would I feel vulnerable in this situation?

All of these last minute frustrations can undo all of the good work that you have been so proud of through your journey.

This is where we use the 6Ps again. Knowing full well that we are going to face this on checking in, it makes perfect sense to have all the information that they are going to need in a pre-prepared travel wallet, along with any 'tip' money etc.

Go and sit in the comfy chairs at reception and take your time filling out the forms, have a drink while you are doing it, take in the ambience, raise your awareness, do I feel vulnerable? No, great.

Get one of the staff to go and check out your door entry card, let them have the stress. They won't have been travelling for hours and hours.

Don't worry about breakfast and all the other bits of information they are bombarding you with, you can sort all of that out in the morning after a good nights rest, safe in the knowledge that you have made it through the whole experience of travelling using the right way of thinking and being aware of your surroundings to the point of not feeling vulnerable at any stage of the trip.

It is important to remember that you are going to have to do this all again in reverse on your journey home, and you would be well advised to plan this before you set off from home before your holiday has started. This will avoid having to spend valuable holiday time that should be for fun and relaxation.

At The Resort/Location

Wherever you are staying it is important to take care of your valuable possessions first before you do anything else.

Make use of the hotel rooms safe if you have one, or go to reception and make sure they place in their safe anything that is of high value to you including your return tickets and passports (make sure you get a receipt).

The only thing that you will need now is the amount of cash you require for the day/evening, your camera or video camera. If like many people these days you are on an all inclusive package, you won't even need cash or credit/debit cards.

While you are relaxing by the pool, beach, on a day trip or excursion it is customary to place everything into a beach bag or holdall. Most of these bags will contain cigarettes, lighters, spare towels, books, spare clothes, every lotion and potion known to man, mobile phones, maybe wallets/purses and lots more besides. But most importantly they will contain the all important cameras and video cameras. People never want to miss a photo or video opportunity while on holiday and will have these items with them all of the time, albeit close by.

I witness people all of the time leave these bags by the pool side, at the beach loungers (or the equivalent) unattended while they go for a swim, fetch food/drinks etc. These electrical items are of high value and very sort after by criminals anywhere in the world, and are very much 'worth their while' taking the risk to steel them from you.

The last time I was on holiday, I was in a resort in Egypt, a beautiful country with very friendly people. I was watching the night time entertainment which was held outside around the swimming pool, all the chairs were laid out in the shape of a theatre. As part of the show the audience were invited to run to the stage area to give an answer to a question. A young man sitting next to me was a very keen competitor and kept running up to the stage to give his answer, leaving his girlfriend on her own. She took charge of the two cameras that they had, and being supportive placed them under her chair so she could stand and applaud her boyfriend. The young man done very well and won first prize. In all the excitement they had failed to notice that their cameras had been stolen. The suspicion fell to the people who had been sitting behind them, three Russian lads who I had noticed earlier in the day, and remarked how suspicious they looked. By the time the couple realised their cameras were missing, so were the Russians, who by now had been picked up from the hotel and were headed for the departure lounge at the airport and on their return journey home. The couple were absolutely devastated that, not only their cameras (worth a total value of over £300) had been stolen, but all the wonderful photos from their trip to the Pyramids had gone with them, as the couple explained to me, for them this was a once in a lifetime trip, they had saved a long time to make this trip happen and without a lottery win would probably not be repeated.

This is a sad but true story, and unfortunately all too common. One moment's loss of concentration is all that is required to have your possessions and memorabilia taken from you.

SUMMERY

A criminal, opportunist or not, will know three things about you when you are on holiday.

1. You are out of your comfort zone and will not have your awareness and concentration levels where they should be, and you will be very easily distracted.
2. You will have high value items on your person, or close next to you at all times.
3. Very soon you will be going home, and you will never meet again.

I have covered many situations and pitfalls when going on holiday where you may leave yourself vulnerable. Some of these may even sound familiar, but because of the very nature of going on holiday, you must have even more awareness of your surrounding and people around you from start to finish. Of course you should have a fun and relaxing time, but you do not want this spoilt or ruined by becoming a victim of crime.

By being aware and thinking in the right way we can avoid so many undesirable situations that we present for crime to happen whilst on holiday.

As always, guard against giving away information about yourself, friends and family to total strangers.

There is a fact of life, very much overlooked, and its simply this: Everybody's favourite subject to talk about is THEMSELVES, so when having conversations with your new found friends, talk about them, what they like to do, where they live, 'who's looking after their house'? Etc. Commit the 6 Ps to memory: Proper Prior Planning Prevents Poor Performance. Make as many check lists as you can, so you don't forget anything.

EXCERCISE

For this exercise, write in the table below, 8 things that you are going to do differently next time you go away on holiday that will make you less vulnerable.

Eight things I am going to do differently next time I am going on holiday.
1.
2.
3.
4.
5.
6.
7.
8.

Once you have completed this exercise, consciously look at your list and ask yourself: Am I using the right kind of thinking? Go over this section again and compare your list until you are confident.

SECTION FIVE

WHAT IS A CRIMINAL?

Why Do They Do It?

WHAT IS A CRIMINAL?

We have so far looked at specific situations and actions that can make us less vulnerable.

This, now, is the most important section in the entire book, to understand 'the enemy' (the criminal).

What Is A Criminal?

To answer this we must first ask what is a crime? The dictionary describes it in this way: A violation of law (serious offence) a wicked or forbidden act, or something to be regretted.

So simply put, a criminal is someone who violates the laws of the land knowingly, with intent or by accident. Confusing isn't it?

As we have discovered, even whilst driving we are all capable of breaking the law at some time or another. For the purposes of this book it is important we concentrate our study on those who violate or break the law with the full intention of doing so.

What Does A Criminal Look Like?

There is very rarely a day goes by without someone asking me 'what does a criminal look like'? Well, gone are the days when a burglar would wear a black beret, black and white stripped jumper, and a black mask across his eyes with a big swag bag slung across his shoulder.

During a training session for one of my security roles, we were shown a large picture frame containing 100 x 1 inch square photos. The photos were of people from all walks of life, everyone from someone who looked like your favourite uncle, a bank manager, Osama Bin-Laden look alike, women, children and anyone else that you care to imagine. We were then asked to approach the picture frame and with a marker pen place a red cross over four of the people we thought looked like terrorists. One by one we done as we were asked. The fascinating fact was, every one of us were correct, every one of the photos were of known terrorists or people who had known connections with terrorism, quite astonishing when you looked at the diverse array of characters on the frame (including children). Using this factual example it is easy to see that a criminal (of any kind) looks like anyone of us, anyone you will ever see, you would never be able to tell.

The Law

We have laws to protect us as a society and as individuals; there are some laws that are so outdated they have been totally forgotten about. Let's take a light hearted look at just a few examples:

The eating of Mince pies on Christmas day is illegal.

It was once also illegal to celebrate Christmas altogether because it wasn't considered puritan enough even though it was a religious celebration.

Do not pretend you are older than you are.

It is illegal to impersonate old age pensioners in the London area of Chelsea.

Your pet should behave as well.

It is an executable offence to allow your pet to mate with a pet of the royal house without permission.

It is illegal to leave your car keys in an unoccupied vehicle.

It is illegal to either shave, work or to mow your lawn on a Sunday.

Tarot card readings and fortune telling are illegal as these are classed as forms of witchcraft.

London hackney carriages must carry a bale of hay and a sack of oats.

The London Hackney Carriage Laws have stayed the same for over a hundred years, and still apply to modern-day taxis. The oats and hay were for the horse, of course. Disputes still arise, and some firms have manufactured tiny bales of hay, so taxi drivers can stay within the law.

Put Stamps properly.

Placing a postage stamp bearing the monarch's head upside down on an envelope is considered as act of treason.

Dying is illegal in the Houses of Parliaments.

A law prohibiting anyone from dying while inside the Houses of Parliament has been voted as the most ridiculous law by the British citizens.

There are of course many other laws that no longer have considerations for our judicial system. It is therefore important that we concentrate on the big three.

Theft
Burglary
Violent Crime

These three crimes are generally the ones that people fear the most. Below are basic definitions of these three.

Theft

Basic definition of theft

A person is guilty of theft if he dishonestly appropriates property belonging to another with the intention of permanently depriving the other of it; and 'thief' and 'steal' shall be construed accordingly.

Burglary

(1) A person is guilty of burglary if—

(a) he enters any building or part of a building as a trespasser and with intent to commit any such offence as is mentioned in sub-s (2) below; or

(b) Having entered any building or part of a building as a trespasser he steals or attempts to steal anything in the building or that part of it or inflicts or attempts to inflict on any person therein any grievous bodily harm.

(2) The offences referred to in sub-s (1)(a) above are offences of stealing anything in the building or part of a building in question, of inflicting on any person therein any grievous bodily harm or raping any woman therein, and of doing unlawful damage to the building or anything therein.

(3) A person guilty of burglary shall on conviction on indictment be liable to imprisonment for a term not exceeding—

(a) Where the offence was committed in respect of a building or part of a building which is a dwelling, fourteen years;

(b) In any other case, ten years.

(4) References in subsections (1) and (2) above to a building, and the reference in sub-s (3) above to a building which is a dwelling, shall apply also to an inhabited vehicle or vessel, and shall apply

to any such vehicle or vessel at times when the person having a habitation in it is not there as well as at times when he is.

Violent Crime

The definition of violent crime suggests that violence is behaviour by persons, against persons or property that intentionally threatens, attempts, or actually inflicts physical harm. The seriousness of the injuries to the victim(s), whether or not guns or other weapons were used and/or whether or not the alleged perpetrator has a criminal record will alter the crimes seriousness.

Confusion

It is easy to see just how confusing all the legal jargon is and even how on many occasions people 'get away with it'. How many times do you hear on the news that someone has received a lesser sentence that does not reflect the crime committed? So, we must ask ourselves, can we totally rely on our legal system, or are we correct in taking steps to make ourselves safer? (This is totally different to taking the law into our own hands). I suspect that you will agree the only way forward is to change our way of thinking and so avoid all of the above.

Why Do Criminals Do It?

The simple answer is: For personal or financial gain, or personal gratification. A more in depth look reveals the following:

There are 7 basic primary reasons for criminal activity:

1) **Necessity:** If you are extremely poor and have to steal to survive.
2) **Opportunist:** While looking at an expensive diamond ring on a jewellery counter and the clerk walks away.
3) **Emotional:** Hate crimes are on the increase and can be associated with this, also "crimes of passion" when a person

kills their spouse or lover are often due to the extreme emotions of the situation.

4) **Ignorance of the Law:** Sometimes you don't even know you're breaking a certain law.

5) **Mental Illness:** Many people who have mental health problems can't truly understand that what they are doing is breaking a law. Often similar to #4 (Ignorance). Can also be less severe like with shoplifting which is often a crime based on emotional issues rather than necessity.

6) **Pre-Disposition:** Some people's personalities and life choices will prompt them to lead a life of crime. Repeat offenders.

7) **Environmental:** If a child grows up believing that certain criminal activity is acceptable (drug dealing, prostitution, cheating on taxes, etc.) it can often enhance their potential for crime. Also, sometimes when people are involved in "group" crimes there are those who really didn't want to participate but only do so because they have a need for belonging.

Does This Mean That Anyone is Capable of Being a Criminal?

Well, Yes. If the circumstances are in someone's favour and they have the opportunity I would suggest we all have the potential to steal at least.

Now before you throw your hands up in sheer horror, let me ask you a question, have you ever sneaked off work five minutes early? Or taken an extra few minutes over a tea break? And not told anyone? (Of course, we all have).

This is time theft. No if's, no butt's, it is a form of theft whichever way you care to look at it, you have stolen time from someone who is paying you for your time. It's theft. No it's not the crime of the century and you may not have even felt guilty when it happened.

There is naturally a world of difference between this and say, stealing someone's car, the difference being that you were pretty certain that you would get away with stealing a few moments from the boss because it was something that was comparatively small, and if you were caught the punishment would only be to make up the time.

Stealing someone's car is much bigger and the consequences are much higher. So, we all have a cut off point, a point where we would not dare go beyond.

Another question, imagine you were walking along a country lane on your own with no sign of anyone for miles, and you happened to notice a carrier bag and on inspection found £2,000 cash in it, all in used notes, what would you honestly do with it? If your answer is hand it in to the Police you would be in a very small minority, if you would keep it for yourself it's another form of theft known as 'Theft by finding' and is an offence. Everyone has a different cut off point from doing right or wrong and very often the decision is made on the spur of the moment. The big difference of course is when a criminal goes out of their way with full intent to break the law and commit their crime.

For every opportunity that we provide for crime to happen (big or small) or a situation to be taken advantage of there will be someone there to commit the crime. This we can be sure of.

SUMMERY

From our perspective of being able to reduce the risk of crime, we have to take the view that, if we provide an opportunity for crime to happen, anyone is capable of taking advantage of the situation.

At the time of completion for this book, there were 7,034,001,734 other people living on this planet.

Let me make it very clear that you are not fighting a single handed anti crime war against the other seven billion plus people sharing the world that you live in. Nor should you have contempt for everyone as being a criminal and they are all out to get you.

You will never change the world, but you can change you.

EXCERCISE

For this exercise, write in the table below 6 times from your past when you stole something (even time) or a time when you were just for a moment even tempted.

No need to write the whole story, just a headline to remind you. It is important here to be honest with yourself, go back as far as you need too.

Six times from my past when I stole or was tempted to steal.
1.
2.
3.
4.
5.
6.

Now consciously look at your list and ask yourself why you were even tempted in the first place? If your answer is because someone had provided an opportunity for you, congratulations, you now understand (albeit on a lot lesser scale) what a criminal is and why they do what they do.

It's as simple as being presented with an opportunity or even being able to create one for themselves because the circumstances were presented right at the time.

Understanding this alone is one of the most important lessons in this entire book and will help you develop your awareness and correct way of thinking to a level you would have never thought possible.

Ask yourself, do I fully understand that by providing opportunities for crime to happen there will always be someone to take advantage of the situation and by reducing these down to a minimum I am protecting everything that I hold dear? If you are not confident, go over this section again until you are confident.

You are now doing fantastic to have come this far, notice the changes in your awareness and correct thinking, hold on to them and start using them all of the time.

You are probably by now starting to see small changes in the way you look at the world around you. Just take a moment now to feel how wonderful it feels to have all of this inside information and to be able to put it to good use.

Close your eyes now and really feel your confidence and power.

SECTION SIX

THE AGE OF TECHNOLOGY

The Technical Bit!!

THE AGE OF TECHNOLOGY

How Far Have We Come?

Never before in the history of mankind has so much technology been available to us. CCTV equipment, alarm systems, mobile phones, computers, the internet, communication devises, surveillance devises, satellite technology etc, the list goes on and on.

We are able to receive information from all over the world instantly at the touch of a button.

The science and technology is increasing and expanding at such a phenomenal rate it's hard to keep up with it all.

We buy the latest, most up to date piece of kit, and as soon as we get it home and unwrap it, something new is already on the market as its latest replacement and on sale next week.

The Truth

While the advancement in technology has, for many people, increased their quality of life, we should consider a simple basic truth. It wasn't that many years ago, say before the invention of the washing machine that the washing had to be done on a certain day and pre-planned.

Nowadays, of course it is common place to do washing anytime, any day of the week. We simply place the washing in our machines walk away and forget about it knowing that it will be taken care of by the appliance we have purchased.

This way of thinking has entered our consciousness for most other items as well. We tend to rely on the item purchased to perform a certain duty for us, assume it will work, and afford it no further consideration. While this gives us greater freedom to do other things, it is dangerous to rely solely on technology when it comes to our safety. Another way of putting it is:

We rely too much on technology and not enough on ourselves.

So many people these days rely on alarm systems, CCTV, tracking devices etc to keep them safe. They have handed over 100% control of their security to something that either has a plug or a battery and truly believe that these things alone will keep them safe.

Any technology is only as good as the person operating it or the correct reaction taking place to it every single time.

All the electronic security devises that are on the market have their place and are there to aid all of our efforts, not replace them.

Alarms

Let's take the example of a car alarm. How many times have you ever heard a car alarm sound and thought to yourself, 'how annoying is that'? No one pays any attention to it, nobody reacts to it and every thirty seconds it goes off again. Now while it is sometimes a good deterrent to a car thief it tends to have, for the best part, an inappropriate response. It's ignored.

There is no alarm system that will keep you safe.

If an intruder, for example, hears an alarm for the first time, it will act as a deterrent. If after the second, third or even fourth time an intruder sees that there is no reaction to the alarm, they will carry on with the crime safe in the knowledge that no one will be investigating it.

Alarms are there to do exactly what they are meant to do. Raise the alarm so that someone will react to it. If there is no reaction, the alarm itself is redundant and is just a 'noise'.

We must meet with technology half way.

You must have a plan in place to react to situations in a correct manner; the same reaction must take place <u>Every Single Time</u>. Many burglars will deliberately set off alarm systems, stand back and watch what happens. This is your weapon being used against you.

CCTV

Closed Circuit Television (CCTV) is a wonderful deterrent and can be seen nearly everywhere we go these days.

I have personally operated and managed CCTV control rooms covering vast areas of public space in all sectors.

To be able to carry out these duties a security officer must hold a PSS (Public Space Surveillance) licence issued by the SIA (Security Industry Authority), Government body, and must have undergone the rigorous training needed to acquire one. CCTV used for public surveillance is usually manned 24hrs a day. The operator will have access to radios linked to security officers or Police officers on the ground. They will be able to direct officers to problem areas immediately allowing for the same level of response every single time.

Under the strictest of procedures, images that are captured on camera can be downloaded onto various formats and used in a court of law to prosecute an offender.

The system works extremely well and is governed by legal actions that must be adhered to in the control room as well as on the ground.

Most homes (and businesses) that have CCTV will not have the same levels of response to a situation as above. They will however have recorded footage of the crime that has been committed, a wonderfully recorded memory of the time and place when they were burgled. Criminals know this and will simply place a hood over their heads so as not to be identified at a later stage. If you are thinking of installing CCTV as a deterrent, consider a dummy system (false but realistic looking cameras) and save yourself a fortune.

Credit Cards

Credit cards are modern technologies way of making transactions and are not without scrutiny from criminals.

Credit card fraud is one of the biggest rising crimes world wide. Below are top tips necessary to keep your cards safe.

- Always check your bank and credit card statements carefully
- Store personal information securely and shred/destroy unwanted documents/receipts
- Be wary of letting your card out of your sight when making a transaction, particularly in bars and restaurants, and especially when abroad
- Make sure you know who you are dealing with before disclosing card details (even to your bank or the police), particularly over the phone or via e-mail
- Never tell anyone your PIN, even if they claim to be from a bank or the police
- Never write down your PIN
- If shopping on-line, use a computer that you know is secure i.e. one with up-to-date anti-virus software and a firewall installed. (Be particularly wary of making a transaction using Internet cafes or public computers)
- Only shop at secure web sites—ensure the security icon (the locked padlock or unbroken key symbol) is showing in your browser window before sending your card details
- Don't use a cash machine if you notice anyone behaving suspiciously around it or you spot anything suspicious on the cash machine itself, always cover the key pad when entering your PIN
- Only take cards that you intend to use abroad and store the rest securely at home. Make a note of your card issuers' emergency contact numbers and keep the information somewhere other than your purse or wallet
- Make sure you get your post redirected if you move house, as your mail is valuable in the wrong hands

What if I am a victim of card fraud?

- Report lost or stolen cards or suspected fraud to your card issuer immediately. The 24-hour emergency number will be on your statement or call directory enquiries.

If you are the victim of card fraud it is likely the most you will ever have to pay is £50. However, if you have acted fraudulently or without reasonable care, for example, by keeping your PIN written down with your card, you will be liable for all the losses.

Mobile Phones

As many as 2,000,000 mobile phones are stolen every year in the UK. Two thirds of the victims are aged between 13 and 16. Many phones are also stolen from unattended cars. Below are necessary top tips to keep your mobile phone safe.

DO

- Register your mobile phone at **www.immobilise.com** keep your phone out of sight in your pocket or handbag when not in use
- Use your phone's security lock code, if it has one
- Record details of your electronic serial number (ESN) and consider separate insurance some phones have an IMEI number which is a unique identifier for the phone; you can obtain this number by typing *#06# (star hash 06 hash) into your mobile phone and it will display a 15 digit number property mark your phone with your postcode and door number to help police identify stolen ones
- Report a lost or stolen phone to the police immediately
- Inform your service provider if your phone is stolen or lost

Don't

- Attract attention to your phone when you are carrying or using it in the street
- Park in isolated or dark areas
- Leave your phone in an unattended car—if you must, lock it out of sight. It only takes seconds for a thief to smash a window and steal your phone.

The security of your portable technology items is the same as for anything else, if you provide any opportunity for a criminal to take advantage of it, they will.

It is absolutely necessary to guard your items well as these expensive products are very highly sought after by criminals as they can easily be sold on for profit.

As fast as technology is advancing, the criminal is working just as hard to overcome any obstacles that technology puts in their way.

A lot of criminals even use this technology to commit their crimes as in the case of computer hackers.

Your mind is the most advanced technological super computer that there is or will ever be. It is therefore with our mind that we must overcome crime and only use mans technology to aid us in our fight, not rely on it alone.

There is no technology that man can devise that man can not overcome.

The battle continues.

SUMMERY

Technology is mans greatest friend, and sometimes his greatest enemy.

When we look at all the advancements we now take for granted as being part of every day life, these things were unthinkable even just fifty years ago.

Most people spend more time trying to figure out how their mobile phone works than they do in training their mind to think in the correct ways to keep them safe in the world.

People communicate via buttons (text and e-mails) far more than they tend to speak to each other. No wonder so many people are providing opportunities for crime to happen more and more.

We rely on technology to do almost everything for us in the modern world, heat our water, cook things in seconds, communicate for us, entertain us, and even keep us safe!

Whilst all this technology is fantastic, entertaining and fun, it will never replace your mind to keep you safe.

Why?

Because it does not have emotion, the gut feeling that something is wrong, the fight or flight mechanism, it can not feel the way you feel. Yes it can make you feel good, but it will never replace the need for human involvement somewhere down the line.

Any technology is only as good as the person operating or programming it

EXCERCISE

For this exercise I want you to write in the table below 6 items of modern technology that have been designed to keep you safe, anything that you can think of is fine.

Here are 6 Items of modern technology that are designed to keep me safe.
1.
2.
3.
4.
5.
6.

Now, look at your list and with each item you have listed, think through all the advantages and disadvantages of that items ability to keep you safe.

Write it out on a separate sheet of paper if you wish. Now do the same with your own mind, list all the advantages and disadvantages of your minds ability to keep you safe.

WOW! That is some discovery you have just made. If you ever needed it confirmed that you have the most amazing piece of equipment that will ever be revealed to the world right with you at all times, in every situation you will ever find yourself in, never left behind or forgotten, right there between your ears, keeping you safe. Listening out for you, watching out for you, guiding you, protecting you, correcting you, and all you have to do in return is feed it the correct information as you are doing. And this is the best part; this brilliant piece of equipment has not cost you one single penny.

SECTION SEVEN

THE MIND

A Place of Discovery

THE MIND

Psychology: The Science of the Mind

Psychology is the science of the mind. The human mind is the most complex machine on Earth. It is the source of all thought and behaviour.

How Do Psychologists Study the Mind?

How can we study something as complex and mysterious as the mind? Even if we were to split open the skull of a willing volunteer and have a look inside, we would only see the gloopy grey matter of the brain.

We cannot see someone thinking. Nor can we observe their emotions, or memories, or perceptions and dreams. So how do psychologists go about studying the mind? In fact, psychologists adopt a similar approach to scientists in other fields.

Nuclear physicists interested in the structure of atoms cannot observe protons, electrons and neutrons directly. Instead, they predict how these elements should behave and devise experiments to confirm or refute their expectations.

Human Behaviour: the Raw Data of Psychology

In a similar way, psychologists use human behaviour as a clue to the workings of the mind. Although we cannot observe the mind directly, everything we do, think, feel and say is determined by the functioning of the mind. So psychologists take human behaviour as the raw data for testing their theories about how the mind works.

Since the German psychologist Wilhelm Wundt (1832-1920) opened the first experimental psychology lab in Leipzig in 1879, we have learned an enormous amount about the relationship between brain, mind and behaviour.

So My Mind Affects Everything Else?

Simply put, yes. You're mind or thinking affects the way you behave at any given moment, you're behaviour affects the way you use your body language and your body language affects the way you think. Its like a never ending circle, one always has an affect on the other. The overall impression is called the emotional state.

The emotional state we are in at any moment can be changed by simply altering your thinking, behaviour or body language.

To demonstrate this, stop and imagine that for whatever reason you care to come up with, you have just lost £50. What is your emotional state (how do you feel)?

Now wherever you are, sit up straight, put your shoulders back, hold your head up, take a deep breath and maintain a big silly grin from ear to ear.

Now think about the £50. If you've done this correctly you will have a totally different emotional state (you will feel different). By just using a small shift in your body language you were able to change the way you were thinking about a bad situation and alter your behaviour towards it.

You can alter any of the three to deliberately make an effect on the other two, and with practice you can achieve this anytime you wish.

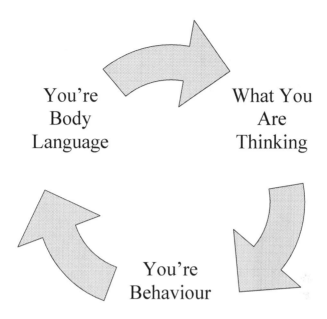

You're Body Language → What You Are Thinking → You're Behaviour →

So With Practice I Can Alter the Way I Feel at Any Given Moment?

Absolutely, this is how we are designed.

I like to look at it this way. We are all have the same electrical wiring in our brains. Imagine anyone you wish tripping over as they walk, what is the first thing they will do? They will put their hands out in front of them to break their fall, correct?

This is true for anyone anywhere in the world; it's a basic human characteristic, of which we all have thousands.

How fantastic is that, not only can we change our own feelings, we can also change other peoples.

As I have said before, any behaviour attracts like behaviour. If you are confronted with someone who is aggressive and you have chosen to be calm and remain that way, they will have no choice but to calm down with you.

If you are walking along at night with someone who is nervous and you have chosen to be confident and remain that way, their fears will diminish. It's the law of human nature.

This is how leaders and followers are formed; leaders tend to be people that have total control over their emotional state at any given moment, not because they feel a certain way but because they have deliberately chosen to feel that way.

The people who do not recognise that they have a choice have no option but to follow.

Now you realise that you have a choice, and that choice is how we think ourselves safe, by thinking, acting and behaving in the correct way all of the time.

Do I Have To Practice Different Techniques?

The more you practice with different techniques the easier it will become.

Let me ask you a question at this point. When you put on a pair of trousers, which leg do you place in first, the left or the right? Did you know, if you were to put the other leg in first you would probably fall over?

Don't believe me try it? Its not something that you even think about is it? You just do it automatically.

There are countless tasks that we all perform every single day of our lives sub-consciously. We are able to perform these tasks without thinking about them for one good reason. We have created a neural pathway in our mind to perform that particular task. The more we perform that task the wider the neural pathway gets.

Let me put this another way, when we learn something new, a different way of doing something or a new way of thinking it is always difficult at first, but after repeated efforts, doing it time and time again it becomes second nature to us to the point where we can do it without even thinking about it.

As far as our studies for our own security and safety are concerned it makes perfect sense to practice the correct ways of thinking and build your awareness as described to a point where this becomes second nature to you. Study all the different techniques in this book, start practicing them one at a time and build your neural pathways to keep you safe at all times.

The Law of Attraction

There is a law of attraction that states: you will get more of what you think about most of the time. Many people have described this in many different ways:

- As a man thinketh so is he
- Man becomes what he thinks about most of the time
- If you hold it in your mind you will hold it in your hand
- You bring about what you think about

The simplest way to describe this is, if you are constantly thinking in a certain way or about a certain situation the chances are that you will manifest whatever it is you are thinking about. If for example you are constantly thinking about being late for a date or a meeting, you will probably be late. Everything seems to happen around you to make you late, everything goes wrong, there is suddenly a stain on your clothes, your shoelace breaks, the hair drier packs up or there is a traffic hold up etc. Does this sound familiar? Of course, because we are thinking in a certain way (of being late) we are bringing these situations into being.

If we think negative thoughts all of the time we are drawing negative situations and circumstances to us.

If we are constantly thinking that we are going to become a victim of crime, our thoughts, body language and behaviour are almost summoning that to happen.

Now the good news is that we are able to turn this on its head. When we are thinking in the correct way, using all the techniques in this book and thinking positive about ourselves and our safety we are calling that into existence.

The relationship between the law of attraction and our mind is in absolute harmony, so if we think we are going to be a victim, we will be. If we think we are going to be safe, we will be. Your way of thinking, your body language and your behaviour will all project the safe image rather than one of a fearful victim.

As we have discovered, we have the ability to think the way we want to think at any given time.

An old colleague of mine, I will call Bob. Bob was what I call a fully paid up member of the 'Aint life awful club' Everything in Bobs life was terrible and of course he was constantly complaining about it from dawn till dusk. He hated his job, he never had enough money, he hated his work colleagues, his wife didn't understand him, he was constantly feeling unwell and the list went on and on. Now Bob's life just seemed to get worse and worse day by day. It didn't matter what you tried to do for Bob he was never grateful and always considered that the world should be helping him because everything was everyone else's fault anyway. Nothing ever goes right for him and he still lives his life in a constant state of doom and gloom. Now you probably know at least one person like Bob, a person that is so negative that everything literally goes wrong for them. The chances are that you also know of one person that is the complete opposite, a person that is always happy, everything always goes right for them, and they literally are having a wonderful life. Some people call these people lucky. It is not luck. It is designed that way, they have habituated ways of living and thinking about the world and the law of attraction is obedient to their thinking and behaviour.

When we use this power of the mind to think and act in the right way, we can keep ourselves safe and free from harm, and when we don't we wont.

To train your mind to reduce the risk of crime and literally *'Think Yourself Safe'* you must study the techniques as described in this book.

Raise your awareness at all times.

Use the correct ways of thinking.

Habituate ways of using your mind, body language and behaviour.

Practice every day, not just as a one time event but all through your life twenty four hours a day.

As I have stated this is difficult at first, but with a little effort it doesn't take to long before you see and feel the results.

You will very quickly notice how fantastic you feel about your ability to reduce crime happening to you and your loved ones. The time to start is now, all this can happen without the need for expensive electronic equipment, an army of bodyguards or an arsenal of weapons.

This my friend is the power of the mind.

SUMMERY

The Mind is by its very nature a hard and deep subject to explore.

I have tried to keep this section as simple as possible and would like to congratulate you on your perseverance with it.

It is important to remember that the mind controls everything that we do.

Our thinking, body language and behaviour. We are able to change all of these at any given time by simply altering one of them as they all feed off each other in a never ending circle. Practice every day to gain maximum effect to a point where correct thinking, acting and your awareness is second nature to you.

Take it slowly at first and try not to run away with yourself, go along at a pace that is comfortable for you. Refer back to this book as much as you need to. Most importantly, enjoy the experience.

EXCERCISE

For this exercise I want you to list the items you are going to practice first in order of your preference.

Plan your training and take each technique or subject and feel comfortable with that before moving on to the next.

My personal training planner.
1.
2.
3.
4.
5.
6.
7.
8.
9.
10.
11.
12.

Practice one subject/technique at a time before moving on.

Feel free to add more subjects or write them out on a separate sheet of paper.

Refer back to your list on a regular basis and constantly ask yourself if you are on the right track, am I thinking, acting and behaving in the right way?

Have I raised my awareness to where it should be all of the time?

SECTION EIGHT

USING THE MIND

Every Day to Stay Safe

USING THE MIND

We have looked at the mind and how we can change our emotional state at any given time.

We are now going to move on and train our mind to specifically reduce the risk of crime in any situation.

We will look at numerous situations where crime is involved and use the techniques and psychology in this book to reduce, thwart and overcome crime.

I would now like to introduce you to **POPS.**

PEOPLE.

OBJECTS.

PLACES.

This is a highly regarded phrase within the security industry and will serve you well. It is a tool of the trade and is learnt very early on in security training and must be understood and memorised to be able to move forward into any sector of the security business.

Therefore I am going to ask you to commit this phrase and its meaning to memory.

We are going to use this tool in conjunction with what you have achieved so far as a new life skill.

PEOPLE

Without people there can be no crime.

We must therefore always be aware of the people around us. There will be those people around us that we feel comfortable with, friends, family, and work colleagues as an example. Then there will be people that we don't know that well, but are also comfortable with, albeit to a lesser degree, such as people in the same social group, are known to have a good reputation, or are generally accepted by your piers etc.

There will be those people that we don't know at all, and as we have discovered we will almost make an instant decision as to whether we feel comfortable around them or not. This will be based on their body language, speech, dress sense, and general persona.

Then of course, there are people we feel threatened by, or feel vulnerable in their presents. This can be one single person or a group, such as a group of hooded youths hanging around on a street corner at night drinking from cans of beer.

Problems occur when we fail to notice the people around us, and this can sometimes be deceiving.

Imagine one of your favourite relatives, the one everybody loves (lets call him Uncle Benny). Uncle Benny is kind considerate, loves life and life loves Uncle Benny. Everyone feels comfortable in his company and he is always the life and soul of the party. That is until he has had one to many whiskies! Then dear old Uncle Benny wants to fight the world. All of a sudden everyone feels threatened by him and no one can control his violent behaviour.

Does this sound familiar, nearly everyone knows an 'Uncle Benny' or indeed an 'Auntie Betty' type character, and unless you know these people very well your guard may be down when the red mist takes hold of them and you could be caught unawares.

It is of paramount importance that we constantly monitor the people around us, all of the time, noticing any changes in behaviour, body language, volume of speech etc.

If we feel threatened or uncomfortable with the people around us we MUST remove ourselves from that situation immediately. Make your excuses and leave, cross the road, get off the bus one stop early, find an escape hatch, do what ever it takes, but remove yourself now.

If the people you are not comfortable with or feel threatened by are on the outside of your home, i.e. suspicious behaviour or anti-social behaviour then call the Police immediately.

Do not confront them yourself.

It is sad to have to say, but people have on rare occasions died trying to face these sorts of people.

The Police have stab vests, sprays, batons and as much back up as they need to deal with the worst case scenarios. Let them deal with it. They are the professionals.

You are not the Police.

People are the perpetrators, instigators and cause of crime. Without people there is no crime.

You will never stop crime happening, but you can reduce the chances of it happening to you.

Your awareness of people around you is possibly your greatest defence.

Make it your number one priority to build your awareness on a day to day basis. Not in a fearful way but in a calm, confident and reassuring way.

OBJECTS

Without objects there can be no theft.

Imagine a world with no objects! Nothing at all.

Wherever you are stop reading and look around you.

Every single thing you have just looked at has been created by man.

As we have discovered, most of these things have been created to make life more comfortable or enjoyable for all.

It is an amazing fact that nearly all the money spent in the world is to make people feel good in some way or another.

Most of this is spent on objects or things that we may not necessarily need to survive but to give us pleasure and the more we have the more we want, and so it goes on.

The more objects a person has the higher their ranking in society appears to be, objects need to be bigger, faster, more expensive and better than anyone else's.

This can create an imbalance between people as individuals or as groups.

Individuals or groups that have very little can become envious of others.

Certain people reside themselves to the fact that they do not have, or never will have the capability to acquire what everyone else seems to have, they then proceed to pilfer objects from those that have them in a misguided illusion that they will feel better about having whatever object it is that they have stolen, albeit for an exchange of money. The thief is born.

There are also people that are so envious of other people's objects that instead of stealing them they damage or destroy what other people have.

Very often in car parks, people's cars will be deliberately damaged. People will walk past a car and run a key along the paint work that costs sometimes thousands of pounds to repair. This only tends to happen to the most expensive cars, or certainly ones that stand out from the crowd, and usually done for no other reason than jealousy or envy.

Criminal damage is an awful thing to happen to any object for whatever reason as the perpetrator is very rarely caught.

Any object can be used as a weapon, not just the obvious like guns and knives, but anything from coins, pens, keys, rolled up newspapers, tools, furniture, to vehicles and anything else that you can think of and in any variety of ways.

The Law describes an offensive weapon in this way: Anything that is MADE, ADAPTED or INTENDED.

That is to say that any object that has been Made specifically to cause harm (such as a knuckle duster). Adapted to be used as a weapon (a piece of 4" x 2" wood with a 6" nail protruding from the end) or Intended (this can be any object at all that is being carried or used to cause harm with the full intent of doing so). Even the Law understands that any object can be used as a weapon.

It is important to understand that objects in your possession or that you own are vulnerable, and the more expensive the object is the more vulnerable it is.

Your awareness must be concentrated on what you have, where you keep it and how much effort is required to keep it safe.

This comes back to your correct ways of thinking.

You must also be aware of objects around you that can cause harm. When you cross the road for example, you will be very aware of traffic for obvious reasons (you don't want to get run over) so it makes perfect sense to be aware of all other objects that have the potential, even in someone else's hands, to cause you harm.

Just being aware of this eliminates the risk by half.

PLACES

Without places there is nothing.

Places are spaces around us that are occupied by people and objects, and there are literally millions of places on earth, most of which we will never visit.

The very first section in this book is 'Your Home' and as I have said, I started with this deliberately because this is the one place on earth that you should be most secure, relaxed and at peace and it is quite right that you do so.

On a scale from one to ten, how comfortable and relaxed do you feel when sitting at home watching your favourite TV programme?

A nice place to be right?

Now imagine that you are at a football match and the game is the most important one for both teams. You are, for what ever reason, the only supporter of your team in the away end of the stadium surrounded by the opposition's supporters; you are dressed in your team's colours and certainly stand out from the crowd. Everyone around you is highly charged with anger because it is your team that is winning with only moments left to play. Suddenly the final whistle blows, your team has won and all eyes are on you.

On a scale of one to ten, how comfortable and relaxed do you feel now? Or indeed how nervous, anxious or frightened?

These two extremes are at either end of the spectrum but there are many times you will have found yourself in places that have given you as much anxiety as the football match example.

It is not the places in themselves that cause the stress, but rather the people in or at them.

Many places are known to be of a volatile nature, or have bad reputations; most towns or inner-cities have certain areas that are best avoided at certain times of the day/night. But it is not always the obvious places that can cause the dangers. It is our inability to be totally focused (as with the example of when we are on holiday) that we leave ourselves most vulnerable.

Any place we could ever go to can be a danger area if we make ourselves an easy target.

In contrast, any place can be made safer by using the correct ways of thinking and acting in accordance to our surroundings at the time. I will reiterate what I have stated earlier:

If you make yourself an easy target, someone will take advantage of you.

This will happen in any environment or place. Wherever you are, wherever you go, whatever you do, it is absolutely paramount that you use your awareness and correct thinking to keep yourself and your loved ones safe at all times.

It is important to take one step at a time. If you try to put into action all of the techniques at once you could experience 'information overload'. As we have found out, we must create neural pathways in our brains (habits) by constant and deliberate repetitions.

I would suggest that you first concentrate on a particular area in your life that is causing you concern, start to think how you are able to use your thinking and awareness to reduce your anxieties or fears. Use the POPs (people, objects, places) tool to help you. If you have any doubt that you are on the right track, read the relevant sections of this book again and again until you feel comfortable.

Once you are confident with what you have achieved move on to another area that has been causing you concern, then take this knowledge into every area of your life, constantly being aware, thinking in the correct way, no longer fearful but confident and self assured that you have the one security devise that will keep you safe at all times, always with you, never failing you, never left behind or forgotten. You're Mind. When this is achieved, you will not be going about your business every day in a constant state of Red Alert, or so stressed out that you can not concentrate on anything else. In fact, it becomes the complete opposite. You will be so hard wire-red that it will be second nature to you, just like putting on those pair of trousers; you won't even have to think too much about it. You will be alerted by your own mind (sub-consciously) that something does not seem right and you're conscious mind will be totally drawn to pay attention to whatever the situation may be and take the appropriate action. You will have freed yourself to be more confident and have a fabulous life.

SUMMERY

Using your mind every day to keep you safe and secure seems like an enormous task at first. This will require a little effort on your part to begin with. Changes will happen very quickly and you will soon have mastered your own fears and anxieties. Remember to take it slowly at first so that you don't become disheartened, and then one step at a time.

As the saying goes, if you want to knock down a large wall, best do it piece by piece, little by little.

Use the POPs (people, object, places) tool to guide you along your mind training journey.

Use your training every single day, and at the end of each day before you go to sleep, reflect on the events of the day and ask yourself how was your thinking? How was your awareness? Have you felt confident in every situation today? If your answers are negative, then think through how you could have done things differently using the techniques in this book.

Refer back to the appropriate section and replay the events in your mind making the necessary changes and how you could have felt so different, and how you are going to make those changes next time.

EXCERCISE

For this exercise, I want you to list twelve advantages that you feel about yourself and your safety since starting *'Think yourself safe'* If you can't think of twelve straight away, then add one thing every day.

Twelve differences I now feel since I started *'Think yourself safe'.*
1.
2.
3.
4.
5.
6.
7.
8.
9.
10.
11.
12.

If you ever doubt that you are doing things in the right way, using the correct ways of thinking, acting and raising your awareness, just refer back to your list of twelve in this exercise, look at all the advantages you have listed.

Use this as your own motivation tool.

SECTION NINE

RESOLVING CONFLICT

When all else Fails!!

RESOLVING CONFLICT

No one ever wants to face a conflict situation, but when all else has failed and you find yourself having to deal with conflict with neighbours, work colleagues, customers or indeed anyone, there are several steps you can take to defuse the situation.

Below are the basic principles used within the law enforcement agencies as standard practice?

There are twelve key points to remember:

1. Space

Everybody has a personal safety buffer zone. This can be affected by personality, culture, mood, environment, situation, gender and familiarity (i.e. loved one, colleague etc). Allow a hostile person plenty of space. Be in a position where you can see them from head to toe. This helps you to judge how they are sub-consciously reacting to the conversation.

2. Stance/Positioning

Avoid aggressive or defensive stances, such as arms folded, hands on hips, waving or pointing fingers or arms and 'squaring' up. Be aware of the message you are sending out. Do not make any sudden movements, relax your hands, breath slowly and deeply and use an opened body language. Stand slightly side on with your hands roughly waist height and your palms facing down. Be aware of the person's body language and posture; are they clenching and un-clenching their fists? Are they pacing about, tapping their fingers, foot or hand? Is there tension around there shoulder or neck, or are they rocking? An individual's culture, ethnic background or gender can all affect the way in which a person can express themselves.

3. Mirroring

It is quite natural for people to sub-consciously mirror peoples actions, mannerisms, gestures and even speech, (particularly people we like). Unfortunately in stressful situations mirroring a person's actions could work against us and usually escalates the situation.

4. Eyes

Make eye contact relaxed to avoid an individual feeling that you are trying to stare them down, as this is seen as a trigger. A good way of maintaining eye contact is to momentarily lower your gaze to their chin and then back to their eyes. Where you look while talking can either be seen as not interested (looking up or either side) or being submissive/victim (looking down).

'If you feel you are losing control and become agitated you will transmit this to the other person and they could become more hostile.

5. Voice

Keep your voice steady, calm and maintain an even tone and pitch. Keep in mind that 38% of communication is tone, so it is not what you say it is the way you say it.

6. Listen

Someone who is angry often needs to 'get it off their chest' and anything that conveys the message that you do not have enough time to listen to their complaint may inflame them further. Re-train your way of thinking and try to think of the person having a go at what you are wearing, not you as a person. To show that you are listening, Para-phrase want they are saying so there are no misunderstandings. Try to create an atmosphere to show you genuinely want to understand their problem and that that you are willing to understand. Show concern and empathy, acknowledge their feelings and acknowledge the need to find a solution.

7. The Environment

The environment in which you are communicating can contain things that will have an effect upon the success of the communication. These are usually obvious although you do not always recognise the effect they are having. These include:
- Loud noise
- Lots of people crowding together
- Physical discomfort—feeling very hot or cold, being hungry or tired.

8. Emotion and Feelings

When you are angry, frustrated or unhappy, the emotions generated will have a direct impact upon your ability to communicate successfully. You find it difficult to hear and correctly interpret words and tend to rely much more on the tone and body language to understand.

9. Alcohol and Drugs

Alcohol has a depressant effect, resulting in slower reactions to normal stimulus. It tends to reduce people's inhibitions and can make them unreasonable and unpredictable. When you are communicating with a person who is under the influence of alcohol:

- Talk slowly and calmly
- Adopt a non-aggressive stance
- Maintain space between them and you

There are many different drugs available and each can have a different effect on the person who has taken them. The effects can range from those similar to alcohol, to high stimulant effects and even hallucinations. The greatest communication difficulty is the unpredictability that can arise in people who have taken drugs and the fact that their world may be very distorted. Remember, drugs and alcohol are often mixed and their effects can be difficult to predict.

10. Cultures Differences

Different cultures hold different values and attitudes to define the way they live and interact with others. There are no 'rights' and 'wrongs' where culture is concerned—one culture is not better than another—just different. Some of this difference may be in things like body language; hand signs in one culture can mean something very different in another, or the difference in space between people when communicating. There are often differences in values, which are difficult to accept. If you want to communicate well with someone who is clearly from a different cultural or ethnic background to yourself, then it is important to respect the values of that culture and try to communicate in a way that embraces those values as much as possible.

11. Mental Health Problems

A person may behave in a certain way because of mental health problems. Mental illness can take many forms. The person may be aggressive for any of the following reasons:

- Fear—(e.g. of noise or of people) leading to desperation and the feeling that 'the only way out is to fight'
- Paranoia—(feelings of being persecuted) may be directed towards certain groups in society, for example Police or Doctors, and could have been caused by bad experiences with them in the past
- Anger—at being provoked by other people, when dealing with people who have a mental illness:
- Give them plenty of space
- Talk clearly and calmly to ensure they understand you
- Make sure they know you mean no harm
- Be reassuring; tell them what you are doing and why
- Keep your hands open and in view
- Reduce distractions that will alarm or confuse
- If you are with someone else, only one of you should talk to the person

Understanding How to Signal Non-Aggression

Signalling Non-Aggression

This is one of the most important areas to understand when defusing a situation where people are becoming aggressive. The more emotional someone is becoming the less they can hear and rationalise what is being said to them. However, they will instinctively respond to body language and tone of voice.

Use the Open PALMS model below to signal non-aggression. It helps you to show another person that you do not want to fight them. Open PALMS = I do not want to fight you.

To help reinforce this model, be confident and give the impression you are capable of dealing with the situation.

Understanding How to Diffuse a Conflict Situation

Defusing and Calming In a high-risk conflict situation the other person is in a very agitated and emotional state and the signals are telling you that you are in immediate danger of being physically assaulted. If it is appropriate, you should remove yourself from that danger.

This is often easier said than done, particularly if you are at work and it is obvious you are in a position of authority and other customers are around who may be left to deal with the situation.

P—Position—allow exit routes, do not block in
A—Attitude—display positive and helpful attitude
L—Look and listen—normal eye contact, active listening
M—Make space—maintain a comfortable distance
S—Stance—shoulders relaxed and turned away to the side

Sometimes, you are not in a position where you can leave easily and safely. Where this is the case, you need to be able to defuse the situation and calm the person down so that he or she becomes less of a risk. There are four basic steps which help to calm a person who is in a high level of agitation and emotion:

- Signal non-aggression
- Catch their attention
- Actively listen and empathise
- Win his or her trust

Signal Non-Aggression

When someone is in a high state of emotion and anger, there is little point in trying to appeal to their rational side. The most important thing to signal is non-aggression—remember 'Open PALMS.' Catch Their Attention If someone has really 'lost it' then it may be necessary to match their level of energy in order to gain their attention. 'Matching' energy level is a delicate balance and needs to be carefully monitored. You need to put yourself in a position where you can gain direct eye contact with the other person and raise your energy and voice to an appropriate level. Use phrases like 'Whoa, just a sec!' or 'Excuse me, can I help?' As soon as you have clearly got their attention, the level needs to drop back to normal and you should maintain the 'Open PALMS' stance.

Show Empathy and Actively Listen

It is quite difficult to stay really angry for a long time and people who are angry respond quickly to anything that sounds like an apology. If you demonstrate empathy with their situation it will help to diffuse their anger. This is not the same as agreeing with them or their point of view—but it acknowledges their right to hold it. You can demonstrate empathy by the use of phrases like:

- 'I'm sorry this has happened to you'
- 'I'm sorry you feel this way'
- 'I can see that this has made you very angry'
- 'I can understand why this has made you angry'

Win His or Her Trust

Winning trust is getting the person to the point where he or she is calm enough to be able to deal with the situation in a rational manner. They have to have confidence that you are 'on their side', want to resolve the problem and have some power to be able to resolve the situation.

Confronting Unacceptable Behaviour

It is important to realise that to confront a person who is already very angry and emotional is likely to escalate the situation and increase the risk no matter how skilled you are in doing it. It is sometimes a difficult choice and it can be hard not to react to some types of abuse—particularly if it is very personal or perhaps racially motivated. Remember that you can confront someone about 'unacceptable behaviour' when it is safer to do so, such as when they are calmer or you are in a safer area. If you feel you have to confront them, then make sure you are assertive rather than aggressive. A good assertive statement will usually clearly state:

- What the unacceptable behaviour is that you want to stop
- What the consequences of continuing will be
- An acknowledgement of the other person's point of view

An example of a good assertive statement is:

'I appreciate you are angry, but if you continue to shout and swear, you leave me no option but to call the Police which I don't want to have to do.' It is important to make sure your body language gives a similar message. You can make a good assertive statement but make it aggressive by 'squaring up' or pointing. Remember 'Open PALMS.'

Recognising and Dealing with High Risk Situations Exit Strategies

When you are in a situation, which you recognize as high risk, it may be necessary for you to exit the situation. This allows you to take yourself out of immediate danger and lets you think rationally about how to deal with the incident. People often find it difficult to get out of such situations without 'losing face' and therefore stay longer than it is safe to do so. An 'exit strategy' is a pre-prepared way of getting yourself away from a difficult situation. You need to have a reason ready so that it comes to mind quickly. It needs to be something that will not make the situation worse.

Law and Where We Stand in Dealing With Conflict

The law relating to self-defence is reasonably clear and unambiguous. However, people often confuse retaliation with self defence. The law does not allow us to retaliate—only to defend others or ourselves from attack.

Use of Force

Authority for the use of force comes from both Common Law and Statute Law. Often it is against the law to use force on another person. Sometimes, however, when justified an assault can be lawful. It is recognising such circumstances that is important. Criteria most relevant in relation to violence at are:

- Defending oneself or others against unlawful violence
- Saving life
- Preventing crime, making a lawful arrest and protecting property

Common Law Authority

Any person may use such force as is reasonable in the circumstances in defence of themselves or others and, in certain circumstances, in defence of property. The force used must be reasonable and no more than is necessary to repel the attack. You must be able to show an honestly held belief that immediate unlawful personal violence was occurring or about to occur and your actions were necessary to prevent such conduct.

In some cases it may be necessary, and lawful, to act or strike first to defend yourself or another person. You must be able to show compelling justification for such action. The law states that some attempt should be made at retreat where practicable.

Reasonable force can also be used in order to save life

Human Rights Act
Use of force must be reasonable and proportionate. This means you must not over-react.

The Act focuses on public authorities, but its principles have a wider influence. Careful consideration must be given to a fair balance between the rights of the person using inappropriate contact and the interests and rights of the community at large. The issue of any physical intervention has relevance to several of the articles including:

- Article 2—Right to life
- Article 3—Prohibition of torture, inhumane or degrading treatment
- Article 5—Right to liberty
- Article 8—Right to respect for private and family life

Article 8 guarantees not only the right to privacy, but also the right to physical integrity, i.e. the right not to be hurt in an arbitrary or unjustifiable way. A lawful interference with a person's human rights must be necessary. This depends upon the measure taken being proportionate to the legitimate goal pursued in respect of qualified rights, like Article 8.

SUMMERY

Resolving conflict can be a very daunting task, it is therefore necessary to understand what is going on, if and when it happens.

This particular section deals with not only your mind but also your body language. It focuses the mind to be at a stage of heightened awareness, so that you can absorb all the information around you at the time of conflict, and to be able to understand all that is happening and most importantly why. Using your body language at this stage is of paramount importance, and used well will defuse most given situations.

No one wants to find themselves in a situation where they are face to face with a conflict situation, but sometimes it is totally unavoidable, say for example if you are at work and dealing with a very angry customer, or anyone you may happen to come across during your day/night. This section will help enormously if used in the correct way. Study these lessons over and over again until you feel confident.

EXCERCISE

For this exercise, I want you to list twelve times from your past where you have had to face conflict, just a reminder of that particular situation will be fine. Write it out on a separate sheet of paper if you wish.

Twelve conflict situations from your past.
1.
2.
3.
4.
5.
6.
7.
8.
9.
10.
11.
12.

Now go over this section again with each of your situations from the list. Think through how each of these situations could have been handled differently by you. When resolving conflict it demands a great deal of self control. By studying this section and replaying scenes from your past with a different outcome will train you to overcome situations should they occur in the future.

SECTION TEN

The Future

Fear of the unknown

FEAR OF THE UNKNOWN

In today's society, we hear more about crime than ever before, murders, attacks, arson, thefts etc. Media coverage of criminal events dominates most headlines. The sociological fallout from all the media's attention is fear. So many people in the 21st century live in constant fear of crime, whether it is being attacked in the street or being involved in a terrorist incident. The media play the biggest part in people's fears, more so than crime itself. The bigger the headline the bigger the newspaper sales and news bulletin viewing figures will be. While the world's media serves us well with information, it is, as always, our own choice whether we are informed or inundated.

Perspective

It is absolutely imperative that we keep a true sense of perspective when we think about crime. Yes crime is there, but crime has always been there and almost certainly in the same magnitudes as it is today.

Strangely enough, we as a society seem to accept crime more than we have done in the past, and the punishment of crime is unquestionably less than at any time in history.

Many criminals appear to almost 'get away with it'. It wasn't so many years ago that criminals were committed to a death sentence for murder or given lashes in public for some lesser crimes. It is really only in what we call modern times that criminals are given punishment of the mind instead of physical punishment. Being locked up for 23 hours a day, having to wear a 'Tag' out on bail, probation, monetary fines and exclusions are all punishment of the mind.

A good friend of mine, an ex-sergeant in the parachute regiment, came to see me one day and explained that he had the most horrendous problem, and he admitted that he was scared for the first time in his life. After a short while he calmed down and explained that he had agreed to be the best man for a mutual friend of ours. As part of his best man's duties he would have to stand up and make a speech in front of 150 guests at the wedding.

This was a man that has jumped out of hundreds more aircraft than he has landed in, seen active service all over the world, been taken prisoner in a far off land, could carry what would to most of us seem like a small house on his back over rough terrain for many miles, and now he has to make a speech was whimpering in front of me with a face like a puppy that had just 'peed' on the carpet.

After trawling through endless sites on the internet we eventually found a best man's speech that he was comfortable with.

We spent many weeks rehearsing in my front room and his delivery on the big day was flawless.

What this, and many scientific studies showed was that people are much more afraid of all things of the mind and a lot less of the physical. I hear all the time that people whilst at work are terrified of getting a telling off for something or another.

We all fear getting embarrassed, told off, made to feel small, losing out on promotion, ridiculed, or most other things that won't physically harm us more that we do things that will.

Rational and Irrational Thinking.

Rational thinking is defined as thinking that is <u>helpful</u> to you over the long run.

Irrational thinking is defined as thinking that <u>hinders</u> you over the long run.

Most fears can be categorised as Irrational. That is to say that they are unreasonable, unfounded and in some cases absurd. That does not mean that a fear to a specific person is not a real fear, it just means that they do not understand what is going on. When we take the time and trouble to understand the things we fear, the fear shrinks to a very manageable state, and in some cases disappears all together.

Most people have a fear, just like my friend, of speaking in public, and it is a very real fear albeit an irrational one.

Once we sat down and studied what was going on, came up with a plan and started him thinking in a positive way and mentally rehearsing different scenarios to overcome his fears he was able to deal with the situation when it came around for real.

This is subconsciously what you have been doing throughout this book. You have been studying what's going on with crime, and you have been doing this with your mind, the same way that society tackles crime in the 21st century, with matters of the mind and not the physical. You are literally confronting the problem 'head on' if you will pardon the pun.

From now on your own internal conversation with crime will be different.

You have learnt how to avoid dangerous situations.

Keep your home and possessions safe.

Drive safely. You have learnt how to prepare and be aware.

You are learning how to listen to and develop your own internal body alarm system (Gut feelings). Confidence is the key.

I have deliberately included the end of section exercises for you to complete because when we put pen to paper we use 100% concentration.

I have also asked you to go over your answers until you are confident and re-check your answers until you are.

I have also asked you to check back on certain exercises if you are ever doubtful that you are doing things in the right way. Look at your own answers to the questions; you have written these for a reason.

This is your very own confidence booster.

All the confidence you will ever need is within you right now, and my one wish is that by studying the lessons in this book it has and will continue to bring your confidence to the forefront of your existence.

The Future

There is a saying that states 'your future is now in your hands' but it is really in your mind.

I have given you a different perspective with crime.

That perspective is that in most cases the victim of crime is 50% to blame. I know what a controversial statement that is and sincerely hope that you are able now to see why.

It is only when we remove or reduce our own 50% through our mental state, awareness and right way of thinking that the other 50% disappears.

Are we able to stop crime happening? No.

Can we reduce the chances of it happening to us? Yes.

Every lesson in this book has been designed to help you achieve just that.

We have looked at the mind in such a way as to create a re-programming that will stay with you forever.

Some of the suggestions have been sub-conscious, and are there deliberately to help you.

Continue to study the subjects in this book, even when you think you no longer need it, never allow yourself to become complacent. As I have mentioned several times, many of the tools are life skills, and that means a skill for life.

Use the lessons well as you look forward to a safer, happier and more confident life ahead.

'May you be safe and protected always'

THE AUTHOR

Tim has been involved in the security industry for many years and has worked with national and international anti-terrorist security units and organisations. He has been part of operations that have procured the welfare of heads of state and world leaders.

Tim lives in Kent in the UK where his involvement in security continues, and regularly advises small businesses and private clients with consultations and presentations.

Lives by the ethos of a 'positive mental attitude' and 'always a little further'.